Dime Stores & Dirt Roads

A collection of short stories.

Dale Forrester

To Ron,
Enjoy!

D1115549

Forres

ISBN: 0615917305
ISBN 13: 9780615917306

Book cover design by: Dale Forrester

Front cover photo: Sonny Forrester and his son Dale
on Carden Avenue in Rossville, Georgia ...around 1961.

Back cover photo: Old Highway 85, just outside
Belle Fourche, South Dakota ...heading toward the
absolute center of the nation.

To Jerrie Sue and Sonny, my family,
and to each and every dog over the
years who decided to stay for dinner

...and then a little longer.

Write it down—that way you won't forget it.

Contents

Prologue

Fall 1970

He made one final turn on the Boston pencil sharpener, grinding his #2 pencil down to its finest point. The sound of wood shaved into a fine writing instrument so fascinated him. He preferred the pencils found in the bookstore, just down the hall on the right. He always chose yellow ...metallics and other odd colorings were best left to the girls. He made his way back to his seat across the light gray tile floors left glistening as if the rain had met them and simply refused to leave. Floors shined with pride by Mr. Foster, the first black man he had ever known. A black man who walked like him, talked like him, and smiled so much that it seemed to be a permanent part of his daily appearance, just as much as his two arms and legs. Surely he was born grinning ear to ear. This boy would learn that he was not that much different from him, it was only a pigmentation issue and nothing more. Mr. Foster made an impression on all the kids, a very significant impression that many kids would carry on with them throughout their lives; some just did not know from where it came. He was a fine man, and his school was always spotless, even the crisp, cream painted block walls shined from his constant care. He had a quiet dignity about him, and he loved those kids.

They loved him too.

The door opened and in walked Mrs. Gray carrying a stack of thirty or so, freshly mimeographed, white sheets of paper. A pop quiz, the most dreaded two words that could possibly be spoken, at least to this sixth grader. A sixth grader who had discovered how enjoyable it was to gaze out the window at crucial points in the lecture and dream of tossing a touchdown pass late in the game to beat the Cowboys, or maybe today he was turning on a Don Drysdale fastball and lacing it down the left field line, ten rows up in the seats. A window, no more than ten feet or so away from his neatly arranged desk and chair combo. The temptation was just too great at times.

She passed the sheets out face down as one by one fellow students displayed looks of worry, confusion and downright disgust as if someone were trampling upon their civil rights. No, most of them did not know what that meant, but they were hearing it a lot on the news at night, and everyone was angry about it. If the people on the TV were angry about it, then maybe they should be too.

Finally, they were instructed to turn the sheets over and begin the assignment, many taking the time to press the bright white paper against their noses to capture the smell left from the ink and pressing of the machine just down the hall. Anxious hearts were thumping, and deep breaths were quietly mixed with the ruffling of the papers. They would soon discover no test questions awaiting them; no discussion challenge, no fill in the blanks, not even a multiple choice. This day, there would be none of that. They would find only an oddly drawn shape with instructions to use their artistic abilities, however crude they may be, to finish and then write a story about their completed piece.

The little boy with the freshly sharpened #2 pencil had found his love.

• • •

I started writing stories back in the sixth grade at Mountain View Elementary School. What began as a simple class assignment from my teacher Mrs. Gray, sparked an interest in me that has been a part of my life in varying degrees ever since. In some ways, I have made my living by writing.

Over the years, I would write mostly for just the shear enjoyment, but, other times, there was just so much more to it. I was simply drawn to a piece of paper at times without knowing why. I would write out of frustration, and during the dark days, I would find solace in the scratching of lead across the sheets. Writing stories to myself would somehow calm me and bring me back to a seemingly balanced point, much like adjusting the sails on the boat while battling a stormy sea as you fight to continue on with the journey.

I would put the pencil down for months on end and eventually those months would run into years. Then suddenly, I would pick it up again; it seemed for no apparent reason, other than I needed to write.

I never kept anything; the writings were too private, so I saw no need in accumulating. I have stated before; while others may talk to themselves or have inner discussions, I chose, at times, to write myself a note. These notes would sometimes be a simple story, maybe a commentary or perhaps an expression of my feelings at the time ...it was just something I did.

This book contains some of my stories over the past year or so. The style, I'm sure, remains the same as that eleven-year-old boy. The crude drawings once used as a stimulus, now replaced with pictures from an iPhone and the pencil, with a keyboard.

If you have taken the time to read this far, perhaps you will enjoy reading just a little further.

I so love to tell stories.

Dime Stores & Dirt Roads

A collection of short stories.

I Kid You Not

I was a late bloomer, as they say.

Entering high school I was maybe an eighth of an inch past five foot tall and weighed in at a robust one hundred pounds. I had reached that much coveted triple-digit mark by downing seemingly every single bag of Golden Flake Sour Cream and Onion Potato Chips that had been placed in the concession at the Mountain View Swimming Pool that summer. I was just a little boy who was absolutely and totally ill prepared for life in this new environment that awaited him.

Now, in my mind I was to be the quarterback as I hit the practice field for that very first day of football practice, despite my increasingly obvious lack of physical attributes. I just knew my tremendous athletic ability, coupled with an astute mind for the game, would be noticed somewhat quickly by the coaches. When they observed the way I carried myself with a game-tested swagger, the fact that I presently could not see over the line would be just a slight inconvenience...a light and momentary trouble if you will. I knew that this seasoned coaching staff would most obviously spot this program-changing athletic specimen and possibly would even place a red jersey on me to protect their prize from taking vicious hits out there on the turf. After all, I was their ticket to the big time. Yep, I was going to pull this train to glory; just hop on boys and enjoy the ride.

I soon found out that this was not to be the case. Much like I would discover a semester or two later in algebra class, my calculations were a just a bit off.

Truthfully, even if I had been six-foot one, I still would have found it rather difficult to beat out another freshman who would start on varsity that year at quarterback and continue on into college. He was tall, lanky, strong, and fast. I was always on time, with my jersey neatly tucked in. He possessed a rifle arm and could take on a truck in a head-on collision and walk away from it. I took directions well, I was very polite, and I rarely fumbled.

Baseball began to look better and better to me.

It's like this—when you see the other boys begin to grow as you're entering your teen years, while you have seemingly plateaued, and you find yourself lagging woefully more and more behind, it truly begins to weigh on you. When your voice isn't changing and the lady at Olan Mills thinks you're a cute little girl, it is downright emotionally devastating. I did not start a growth spurt of any kind until I was fifteen ...I even grew an inch or so after high school.

Now, everything I have told you so far leads you up to a specific event in my life. A red-letter day that would actually occur a good seven to eight months prior to my quarterback tryout. The date would be December 23, 1972. But, before I explain the significance of that day, I need to back up just a bit more.

We lived in a ranch-style house when I was growing up, or at least waiting to. There were hundreds of variations of the ranch-style design throughout the many streets and the abundant hills of our neighborhood. I loved ours because it was all brick and seemed to be kind of in the middle of all the other houses.

There was one thing that was fairly consistent in those days ...eight-foot ceilings. Ceilings that I simply could not touch no matter what technique I chose to use. I would run down the hall as fast as I could and thrust myself upward and draw nothing but air. From the standing position, I fared no better. At that time, I'm figuring the measuring stick had me around an inch or two less than that much-coveted five-foot goal of mine.

Before I take you back to that December day, please note that I had made this leap to touch those "popcorn" ceilings most likely hundreds of times ...basically, each and every time I walked through that house for at least the past two years. In essence, from the very moment that I thought there was even the slightest chance I could graze them, I became obsessed with it. I had to be coming close on some of my attempts, I just knew it. After all, Mama told me so, and she wouldn't tell her baby boy that if it wasn't true.

3

Now, back to December 23, 1972. Christmas Eve Eve, a Saturday to be exact. In two weeks I would turn fourteen.

I'm sitting sideways in Mama's orange Naugahyde chair with our poodle, Bridget. Don't even get me started on how much I loved that dog. This was the customary position I would find myself in anytime I was going to watch a ball game. But please, trust me on this one, this was no ordinary game. This, my friend, was an AFC divisional playoff game. We're talking the beloved Pittsburgh Steelers against the much-despised Oakland Raiders. It was right versus wrong. It was good versus evil. The Raiders had Jack Tatum, and the only person I despised more than Jack Tatum would have been Mama Tatum for having the absolute gall to birth him into this world. This was more than a sixty-minute tussle on the turf. This single event could change the course of further human events in my mind. The Steelers *had* to win this one.

Most likely I had a bag of Ruffles with me. I'd eat two, Bridget would eat one. I also recall Dad sitting across the den from us. Like me, he was pulling for the Steelers ...he was a Terry Bradshaw and Steel Curtain man. I pulled for Terry Bradshaw as well, along with whoever was playing against Jack Tatum and that evil empire of darkness known as the Raiders.

The game kicks off midafternoon, and it's cold and spitting snow in Pittsburgh. Truthfully, when I was a kid watching TV, it was always cold and snowy in Pittsburgh ...I'm thinking pretty much year-round. In fact, I think I once saw Willie Stargell take one deep off Vern Ruhle in a driving snowstorm in mid-June at the old Three Rivers Stadium.

Curt Gowdy was doing the play-by-play, as he did for every single baseball and football game on the tube back then. It was like he could be working a game in say, Baltimore, and then when it was finished, he would show up immediately across the country announcing the game in San Diego. He liked talking so much that he did the play-by-play on hunting and fishing shows in the off-season, for goodness' sake.

Dang, I loved Curt Gowdy.

The game itself was a slugfest to say the least, and if you liked defense, you were loving it. The Steelers were up just 3-0 going into the fourth quarter, and I'm thinking, could they possibly win this thing without even scoring a touchdown?

The Steelers would kick another field goal, and now my confidence begins to build. Let's finish this thing ...send the silver and black back to Cali and shut their mouths for another year.

Then the unthinkable happened.

As if scripted from a horror movie, Ken Stabler drove the Raiders right down the field in the closing moments: an agonizing drive that he finally capped off by taking it in himself from thirty yards out for the touchdown. It was as if he punched me right in the gut. A minute to go, the Raiders lead 7-6. It was all but over, the unthinkable was about to occur. All hope was lost. Christmas would obviously be ruined, and you just know there weren't enough turnip greens and black-eyed peas on the grocery shelves to rescue this great country from the economic doom that surely awaited us in 1973.

I could just picture Jack Tatum laughing and making plans to visit his buddy, the mean one, Mr. Grinch, to celebrate the holidays.

The Steelers got the ball back, and after a few feeble attempts, they were facing a fourth down ...a good sixty yards from the goal line with mere seconds remaining. The pain and anguish was slowly consuming me as I hugged a despondent Bridget. I knew that soon I would be in the fetal position with her. She always took a loss so hard.

Here we go, possibly the final play of the game for the Steelers. Terry Bradshaw takes the snap and drops back. He looks one way, then back, and then heaves one over the middle about twenty yards downfield to Frenchy Fuqua coming across. The ball was not a tight spiral, but it was heading right toward the target when suddenly out of the black clouds that dastardly Jack Tatum arrives just in time to place a hard hit on Frenchy and deflect the ball back five yards or so in the other direction toward the AstroTurf ...game over.

But wait!

Somehow, Franco Harris arrived like the cavalry on the old western plains, plucking the ball just mere inches from the turf. He is now scampering untouched, down the remaining forty-two yards toward that blessed goal line ...the winning touchdown. The crowd goes crazy, Curt Gowdy just about loses his golden voice, Bridget begins howling at the top of her lungs, and at that very moment, I let out a scream as I leapt up from that orange Naugahyde armchair upward toward the sky, only to be stopped with my hand firmly pressed against that elusive popcorn ceiling.

I kid you not.

I came back down to earth just as the refs are trying to figure out what happened. We're talking some serious pandemonium here. Curt is now delirious, Al Derogatis, his trusty color man, is trying his best to make sense of it all, while I am now totally convinced that I may have just acquired super powers.

Finally, after much deliberation and many prayers finding their way through to the heavens, the referee, Mr. Fred Swearingen, stepped to the middle of the field and signaled touchdown. The Steelers would win 13–7. Goodness and the American way had indeed prevailed.

Yes, I saw it all...I didn't miss a second. I witnessed what is now referred to as the most famous play in NFL history, the now-legendary Immaculate Reception.

However, at that precise moment in a brick ranch-style house resting in the hills of Mountain View, a young man had had an equally startling experience ...my very own Immaculate Elevation.

It would take several more weeks before I was finally able to simply touch that ceiling again on one of my many daily jaunts down that hallway into the den.

I kid you not.

Leaving a Mark

"Suppertime!"

The stern, motherly voice bounced throughout this cozy neighborhood of box houses, rows of homes lined with oaks and maples and dreams and hopes of a better world than the one these moms and dads had grown up in.

She was playing with some of her friends ...possibly they were just talking and giggling on the wall near the school just down the street from supper ...a child of the forties. The war had just concluded, and in some ways we were still clinging to our innocence. The exact time it would leave us is hard to say, but it would one day leave. Oh, yes, it would.

This smiling little second-grader probably met her little brother on the way back to the house. An older sister was helping with supper, while the remaining sisters had each married and were now having children of their own ...some near the age of Jerrie Sue and Larry.

Supper was most likely uneventful. They sat at a table bookended by a father who often smelled of an odd mixture of burnt metal, Camels, and "cough syrup" and a mother who not only bore him six daughters and finally a son, but always waxed her floors on Saturday ...every Saturday.

The last of the cornbread and buttermilk is lapped up ... plates are being cleaned and stacked, and the kids run out to catch just a little bit more of the daytime that's left.

She has no more than skipped out of her yard when she hears a scream ...a tone in a voice that pierces her name into the pink skies that are painting themselves just past the oaks and maples. There's trouble at home, and she has been summoned.

Today I have a nightstand, a lovely piece of furniture that belonged to my grandmother, my mother's mother. A lady I never got to know—she passed away in 1964. She was a classy lady from what I have gathered and dressed like a fifties sitcom mom at all times. You're thinking sweet and loving thoughts right now, but I would be remiss if I didn't let you know that a major portion of her blood was Cherokee, and she knew very well what a warpath was and how to get there. By all the accounts I have heard over the years, she could get there very quickly at times.

As for the nightstand, it has retained its beauty all these years. It's still good for holding a lamp in front of a window or perhaps your prized collection of those highly sought-after Precious Moments figurines. A very classic style that I still see every once in a while at various antique stores.

I recall my mother telling me of only two whippings she received as a child. One was the time she discovered her father's ...oh, let's go with uniform, from a certain society he belonged to. She tried the face covering on just as he was coming around the corner from the kitchen. It was at that precise moment that she would receive what she often referred to as the beating of her life.

The second time was about to occur.

My mother had witnessed some boys carving their names in desks at the school, a perfectly normal practice back then. Truth be known, when I graduated from Rossville High School, I had left my moniker in several pieces of wood throughout the campus. It would seem by the etchings in various desks that several famous movie starlets of that day were indeed in love with me. I would be reminded of this fact by various students who followed me for years at that fine institution of learning. Nothing says love like the permanence of wood carving in my book.

The little girl sheepishly entered the back of the house, trying to quieten the screen door as it squeaked and prepared for its inevitable meeting with the frame. A sound that a true southerner loves to hear ...but not this true little southerner, not this time. She was hoping that lessening the sounds of the moment would somehow, in turn, lessen the tension that she most assuredly felt as she walked past what had been a loving dinner table no more than three minutes ago and onward toward the living room.

There, in front of the picture window, stood her mother in full tribal mode ready to inflict grave danger upon the person who had carved an initial into her beautiful and now, it seems, priceless nightstand. I can almost see the glare and feel the venom all these years later, and the wrath that incurred is one that this little girl, my mother, would speak of only sparingly and in hushed tones for the rest of her life.

Ironically, my mother had made her mark, and now my grandmother would in turn make hers and thus end a possible thriving wood carving career that very night.

I thought of this story tonight as I walked past that night-stand ...that very nightstand that now proudly sits upstairs at my house, under a window, holding a lamp ...a job it has done very well now for a good eighty years or more.

I love that mark, and I'm not ashamed to say I rub my fingers over it often.

Miss you J.

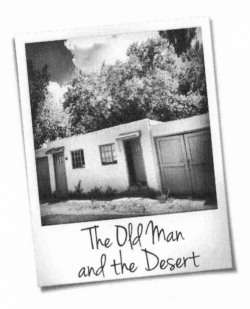

The Old Man
and the Desert

Have faith in the Yankees, my son.
Think of the great DiMaggio.

—The Old Man and the Sea

I have read *The Old Man and the Sea* twice. The first time, it was just so I could say I did. The second time was because I was still tasting the saltwater from the first reading, and I had a hankering to get back into that boat.

Ernest Hemingway wrote the book in 1951, as history tells us, while living in Cuba. Simply put, it's the story of an old fisherman named Santiago who has had such a long string of bad luck on the sea that villagers shy away from him ...considering him *salao*, the worst kind of unlucky. He is befriended by a young villager named Manolin, upon whom Santiago imparts

13

wisdom. This wisdom includes, of course, fishing and the New York Yankees, Santiago's only passions.

Santiago soon makes the decision to sail out into the Gulf one last time to break his unlucky streak. It's here that the novel takes you through every painstaking twist and turn of a lonely old man, trying to salvage his name and create his legacy with perhaps this, the final catch of his lifetime.

The book can at times make you feel as though you are actually sitting in the boat as Santiago takes that last journey out to sea ...a journey for which I'm sure Hemingway found inspiration from his time in Havana and the various seaports in and around Cuba during the pre-Castro days.

I love the book, and I've always had a fascination with Hemingway.

A few years ago I got to visit Key West for the very first time. I saw beauty, I saw some crazy things, I listened to some great music, and yes, I most certainly experienced Duval Street ...I did it all. I love everything about Key West, but my favorite part of the trip was taking a tour of a beautiful old home that sits at 907 Whitehead Street. The home is sixteen feet above sea level, somehow I remember the guide telling us that, but it's still the second-highest point in Key West. It was built in 1851, but it would become famous later on as the home of Ernest Hemingway.

I saw the six-toed cats, I saw the old urinal from Sloppy Joe's that he had converted into a water fountain, and I saw his typewriter. The typewriter rests upstairs in a small house adjacent to the main living quarters. It sits just as it did so many years ago, awaiting a master to call upon it to craft words of elegance and steel. But today, it sits there silently. This very typewriter at this very place where Ernest Hemingway would have to stand to type his masterpieces because his back hurt him so.

Ernest Hemingway could make Chuck Norris shake.

Recently, some buddies and I were making the cross-country journey from Chicago to Santa Monica by way of the old Route 66. We were traveling through yet another uneventful stretch when we ventured up on what was basically a ghost town ...a town by the name of Cubero, New Mexico.

Now, if you've never taken the trip across the Mother Road, you must realize there are many places that you will pass through, or by in some cases, that at one time used to be something. Truthfully, there are times that you look around and you just don't see how an area could have at one time possibly been thriving.

Cubero is in essence a rundown vacant building on one side of the road and another across the street, which has been converted into a convenience store with four or five seemingly vacant little box houses behind the store. That's the entire town.

Yes, it is quite obvious that Cubero has seen better days.

We got out and kind of looked around and then walked across the street for some refreshments.

To me, the little town looked like a pretty good spot for a music video. I could picture a fifties model pickup truck sliding into the dirt parking lot there by the gas pumps, stirring up the dust while some lovely girls in cowboy boots and flowery cotton dresses walked slowly around for no apparent reason. Now, while all of this is occurring, our hot act du jour is strumming on his latest country hit. I'm picturing him to be a hat act, with a pearl-snapped western shirt—possibly with the sleeves cut off—and of course Wranglers and cowboy boots. To top it off, the sun will be setting in just a few hours, so we can get a really cool shot from behind of him walking toward the glow, guitar in his right hand, as we fade to black ...and *cut!* One more thing, we need an armadillo—somebody get on that ASAP.

Back to the real world.

We entered the store. I grabbed some water and a candy bar, and I then noticed lots of old pictures adorning the walls. Some were of famous movie stars back in the thirties and forties. I was totally intrigued.

After further investigation and also after overcoming a slight language barrier with the present proprietor, we found out that this was once a tourist court, café, and trading post dating back to 1937. It was so popular that when Lucille Ball split with Desi, she drove over here and stayed for a while. Now that's an interesting tidbit for you.

But wait, here's another shocker. Around 1950 or so, it seems a man rented one of those small bungalows out back while he was working on a project. That project was a book, that man was Mr. Ernest Hemingway. The book? You guessed it, *The Old Man and the Sea.*

I just stood there for the longest in stunned silence. I looked around and got to thinking that maybe with some soap and water, several cans of paint, a really good sign out front, and then maybe a clever website, we could have ourselves the making of an absolute, good old-fashioned tourist stopping point. It's called marketing, my friend, and believe me, there are folks out there making lots more out of a whole lot less on the old Route 66 trail.

But something tells me that's just not going to be happening anytime soon.

So, there you have it, in the absolute middle of nowhere, in a long since abandoned and somewhat forgotten little town, greatness visited on more than one occasion.

It kind of reminds me of a line from a Guy Clark song...

"There's a lot more standing here than what you see."

Yep, Cubero has indeed seen better days ...but then, haven't we all?

The Soon-To-Be Legendary Jesse Taylor

I got in late Sunday night from the 30A Songwriters Festival down in Seaside, Florida. Yes, a good time was had by all, and I learned a few things over the past week.

For starters, crowd surfing is really frowned upon. Not only is it frowned upon, but also from what I found out later—as I was getting up off the ground while simultaneously being beaten by two angry old women with their purses—it had never even been attempted in the entire history of the 30A Songwriters Festival.

Also, shredding and wailing is not about lettuce and hunting mammals found in the sea. Shredding is the act of absolutely wearing a guitar out. I mean working your way down to the last few frets, which I thought were just there for looks. You do this to the absolute delight of throngs of adoring fans.

Wailing—now, that is the act of just rearing back on vocals and letting it fly. I was privileged to witness both at their finest.

Finally, I still got it ...more of it than I should have in some places, but I still got it. I can hang out with the hip people and get crazy while my new hero and bud Matthew Sweet absolutely shreds and wails. I can sing as loud as I want, chill with some famous people, and basically be the honey badger all weekend long.

Yep, there are times when I really love being me.

I was dead tired as I dropped my bag in the kitchen and began to check the mail. I headed to the fridge and then noticed a big envelope propped up near the canisters ...a big envelope not only addressed to me, but from Hawaii of all places.

I opened it up, and inside was a note, along with two tickets. Not just any two tickets, I will have you know, but two tickets to see George Strait next month in Atlanta. It was a gift from an old friend—a gift from a young friend, actually, but one much wiser than his years—my very good buddy, Jesse Taylor.

Jesse is a wonderful singer/songwriter from the great state of Washington who now lives in our fiftieth state (by the way, it's beautiful, Jesse, but get your butt back to the mainland). Jesse cannot only pen beautiful and classic-style country songs but will sing them anytime, anywhere, day or night ...trust me. If you like your country more old school, then do yourself a favor and download his new album *Out Here in the Country* on iTunes ...I recommend it highly.

The picture above was taken the night we hopped into a brand -new black Mustang Cobra—Jesse, my son Corey, and me—and burned the asphalt (as much as I can burn), all the way from Austin, Texas, to one of the most special places on this here planet Earth: the legendary Gruene Hall in New Braunfels, the oldest dance hall in the great state of Texas. I've written about it before, and I promise I could write volumes more. By the way, notice a young George Strait in the picture behind Jesse's left shoulder. Mr. Strait has played at Gruene many times.

This night was a reunion of two young men who had met by chance in Yellowstone National Park a couple years ago. A chance meeting that would soon lead to a cross-country trip in an old Ford pickup truck with no timeframe and no plan other than to get to Nashville. They had a long way to go and all the time in the world to get there—a trip they would embark on with just a few dollars in their pockets, Jesse's guitar, and a box of his CDs, which they would sell at various stops and impromptu concerts throughout the west. Oh yeah, the other young man in this newly formed partnership was my son, who can charm and sell snake oil to the very guy who turns around and sells ice to the Eskimos.

This trip would start at the edge of the park, somehow head west through Las Vegas into California and back over into Cody, Wyoming, down toward Amarillo, Texas (by morning thank you). They kept heading eastward and somehow eventually slid into the loveliest of all towns, Chickamauga, Georgia, some two weeks later.

Along the way, they made 437 new friends, slept in the truck on more than one occasion, and a few nights they slept on the front porch of some new and dear friends they made in Wyoming. They stood on a corner in Winslow, Arizona, met Elvis, snuck into more than one hotel breakfast bar, and met two lovely girls on the Vegas strip who they would, surprisingly, find out several blocks later were actually "working" ...if you know what I mean. Along the way, they would fill that pickup truck full of stories.

Trust me, I've heard a sampling of those stories, and Hollywood only wishes they could write stuff like that.

I got to watch this reunion of friends ...true friends, or as we say around here, "Two a.m. friends." Lord knows those kind are rare and so very special ...you collect 'em like diamonds, and they are far more valuable.

Jesse sent me those two tickets in appreciation for that special night at Gruene Hall. I sent word back thanking him for them, but truthfully, he didn't need to thank me at all.

You see, I got to sit there that night on a bench and listen to the Dirty River Boys bring it, and I mean bring it hard. I got to watch two young men continuously laugh and genuinely enjoy each other and their time together at an old and faded, slightly less than plumb pool table, while the neon-infused ancient wood walls glowed in yellows, blues, and reds. I got to see and hear the rain as it presented itself steadily outside the screens just a few feet from us ...a rain that the locals greeted with cheers as the skies opened up that night and poured down long-awaited and much-needed moisture. In all of my years, I had never seen precipitation get a standing ovation. I soaked it all in while music filtered the air like flowers in the spring, and thankfully I was well aware at the time that I was in the midst of one of those pinch-me moments.

Oh my gosh, oh my gosh.

I got to be a part of a moment in time that surely the good Lord will never, ever let me forget. I don't think the boys will forget it, and something tells me their grandkids won't either.

Thanks again, Jesse.

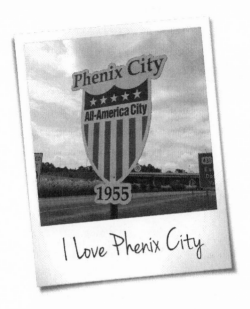

I Love Phenix City

Drove through the lovely town of Phenix City, Alabama, yesterday, just across the state line from Columbus, Georgia.

Now, Phenix City is a nice little place. In fact, it's the hometown of one of my all-time favorite high school coaches, Coach Mayo. I used to ask him all the time where he was from, just so I could hear that distinctive accent. His rendition of my last name in a slightly disgusted manner remains one of my all-time favorite versions. To this day, I can close my eyes and hear it most anytime I want.

As I headed out of town there on 280, I noticed a billboard on my right. The board fascinated me so much that I turned around and went back to study it some more. In fact, I studied it so much that I finally got out and took a picture ...I simply needed to document the fact that Wanda "The Bang Bang Lady" was running for county commissioner. I then looked her up on the Internet to find that not only was she running for the District 7 county commissioner seat, but she also owned a local fireworks store right there in Phenix City, a very successful one too. I suddenly became a fan of the Bang Bang Lady, and I believe you will too if you visit her website at www.bangbanglady.com.

Yep, I love me some Phenix City.

Here's another tidbit for you. One night, several years ago at the Pizza Hut in Phenix City, I witnessed a truly bizarre event. As I sat there with the family, at this kind of midway stop on our way back from our latest Florida adventure, in walked a group of about ten happy folks. The waitress scurried about and put together several tables for them right next to us. They were a pleasant group, obviously locals, and upon casual inspection they appeared to be wearing their Sunday best. I soon picked up from their conversation that they had just visited the local funeral home. Now, one particular fellow, sitting at the head of the table, was wearing a navy suit and black penny loafers with white socks, and he was by far the most vocal in the bunch. His accent was extremely distinctive ...think Larry the Cable Guy, but not as refined and polished. He loved to rise up off his seat as he made animated hand gestures, delivering his courtroom-style points throughout the various discussions. They were a loud bunch, having a wonderful time.

It was a perfectly normal Sunday night in the Deep South.

Now, I was born in the South, I was raised in the South, and yes, I will die here one day. The southern accent and all its variations is an absolute thing of beauty to me. Many people equate it with a lack of intelligence, but I will stand and tell you that some of the more brilliant people I know seemingly do not possess a one-syllable word in their entire vocabulary. One of my very good buddies, who stands upward of six-foot-five, famously quoted in a meeting with some blue-suited executives, "Boys, don't let these overalls fool ya." Truthfully, I rank him as one of the smartest individuals I have ever known.

Back to the Pizza Hut.

The aforementioned gentleman in the blue suit, white socks, and black penny loafers was making another one of his many grandiose points when he turned his head slightly, and it was then that I noticed something. That slight turn of his head revealed seemingly a perfectly round bald spot for just a split second, and for some reason, this struck me as a little odd. Obviously a bald spot is not uncommon, but his seemed to be a perfect circle. I looked back to my plate just as quickly and went back to minding my own business. Then, once again, he turned, and it was at this moment that I dropped my slice of thick-crust sausage, pepperoni, and mushroom down onto the plate. That, my friends, was no bald spot—that, my friends, was a ~~yamaka,~~ yarmulke ...I had unknowingly stumbled upon what was most likely the only Jewish good ol' boy in all of Phenix City, Alabama.

I simply did not see that coming.

I sat there absolutely stunned the rest of the night as we munched on pizza and just enjoyed ourselves. I could easily hear him laughing, cutting up, and just doing what us southern people do. I'm telling you, the guy was the life of the party. I lovingly nicknamed him Billy Bob Goldstein.

I said all that to say this: in honor of Helen Gurley Brown's ninetieth birthday today, be sure to vote for Wanda "The Bang Bang Lady." Think about it—a hundred years ago or so, women couldn't even vote, and you certainly couldn't wear your ~~ya-maka,~~ yarmulke to the Pizza Hut in Phenix City, Alabama.

Yep, we live in a great country in spite of what you may have heard or read in recent years.

God bless Phenix City, God bless Coach Mayo, God bless Billy Bob, and you go get 'em, Ms. Bang Bang Lady.

Girls' Night Out

I was riding through the cove a few evenings ago in my Jeep with the top down ...I so love doing that. It was at that perfect time of day, you know, those precious few moments when the sun is slowly beginning to leave us for a while and wants to show off just a bit before bidding us adieu. The sweet amber glow from this "golden hour" gives everything it touches a new perspective ...a softness and hue that seems to slow time down to a three-quarter beat for the final dance of the day. Beauty is beauty, but beauty at this time of day becomes even beautier. Yep, that's my word, feel free to use it.

As I came up on a little hill into a slight curve, I spotted a gathering just up ahead and to the right. I immediately felt the overcoming urge to pull over and investigate. Yes, I guess I was being nosy, but I simply just had to check out what could be causing such an obvious commotion.

I hopped out of the Jeep, and as I made my way to the gate, I realized this was no random gathering ...it's Friday, and this was Girls' Night Out. Not only that, but what in the world is a guy like me doing interrupting them? A faux pas, I must say, of the highest order.

Since I had already gone this far, I went ahead and approached the gate and humbly apologized for my rudeness. The ladies were extremely gracious, and I then informed them that they had never looked more enchanting—that's right—and I'll even go so far as to say even beautier than ever ...you know, that whole golden-hour thing.

I then asked if I could be so bold as to perhaps take one picture to preserve this magical moment for future generations to gaze upon. Just one snapshot and I would be on my way. Through sweet giggles, they somewhat blushingly agreed. Yep, even cows love to hear how pretty they are.

The girls gathered together for a somewhat informal group pose, each complaining they needed just a little more primping time. I then felt the need once again to assure them of their absolute loveliness.

On three, I told them to say cheese, which I immediately found somewhat ironic. They each got a big laugh out of that one as well, and it was then that I snapped my picture. I thanked each of them, and we all went about our business on this, yet another lovely Friday evening in north Georgia.

I hopped back into my Jeep, but I couldn't help but look back one more time at the girls as they now headed on toward a hill, back up into the pasture. They seemed so happy to be together as they made their way calmly through the lush, hoof-deep landscape. You know, there are a whole bunch of people in this world who never get to see sights like this ...I am truly a blessed man.

I pulled out of the gravel and slowly drove on through the winding roads with the sun gently escaping behind the mountains. It was then that it occurred to me ...we don't tell the ladies enough just how pretty they are. We just don't. Truthfully, every single girl deserves to hear it.

Especially when she looks even beautier.

The Pope, the Dog, and the Packer

There was a picture that hit the news and made its way across the Internet last year that grabbed my attention immediately. The picture was taken in Guanajuato, Mexico, and it shows a cobblestone street thoroughly lined with well-wishers all excitedly cheering on a perfectly shocked and absolutely amazed little dog. I swear you can almost see those emotions on his face as he makes his triumphant stroll basking in the love of the throngs.

Truthfully, they were not there for him.

On this day, Pope Benedict was visiting the area on his way to Cuba, and his motorcade had just passed by only moments before the shot was taken. Our unknowing dog was simply walking down the street behind the cars, minding his own business, when suddenly the cheers and outpouring of love once directed to the Pontiff were now being directed at the most surprised canine in all of the world.

He had no Westminster dog show award and no registration papers I'm most certain could be found. He likely was from the most modest of backgrounds, but for this moment, this little dog absolutely mattered.

That picture still totally does it for me. I wish I could show you, but I would have to trade my house to the proper folks for the rights. Thankfully, you can pull it up rather easily on the Internet.

The other night, I was scanning the TV rather late, looking for some thought-provoking and mind-stimulating programming. I ended up on one of those obscure triple-digit channels just as two boxers were being introduced, mere seconds before the bell would ring to start their contest.

Now, I'm not going to give you their names simply because to my horror, they could somehow do a Google search, perhaps get offended, and bring their professionally licensed fists to my lovely and quaint little town. I will say this however: one of the fighters was nicknamed "The Packer," and the other one, unfortunately, didn't possess a catchy moniker, so we're going to go with "Chubby Mexican Dude." It was to be a four-round fight and, after hearing their bio information during the ring introductions, which by the way I feel most certain, was not taken from their LinkedIn accounts, I felt compelled to watch the outcome of this contest of fisticuffs ...and you will soon see why.

The bell rang, and the Packer and Chubby Mexican Dude proceeded to give it everything they had. The crowd was totally into it. Leather was being traded, sweat was pouring, and pugilistic skills were truly on display for the excited throngs to enjoy.

All right, maybe I'm exaggerating just a bit. To be totally honest, the way these guys were tossing punches around, they were fairly safe inside that ring. As a matter of fact, I'm thinking the ring girl would stand a good chance against either one of them if she would simply stay outside and keep working the jab.

Finally, the bell rang, mercifully ending the contest after that fourth and final round.

As the fight ended, they each held up their gloves, signifying their absolute certainty that they had indeed won this hotly contested brawl. However, we soon cut to the ring announcer, who has the judges' official opinion. After four rounds of boxing, the judges have reached a unanimous decision ...ladies and gentlemen; we indeed have a winner ...in the blue corner, the Packer!

Upon hearing this glorious news, the Packer proceeds to jump up and down ecstatically, and then he does a few of those fighter poses for the cameras. Hey, he's working his way up the boxing ladder, and surely there's a championship fight on the horizon. You just know he's got a big payday waiting on him down the road. As the microphone is placed in front of our gallant victor, he humbly begins to tell the lovely lady reporter in the ring, as well as all of the totally engrossed viewers across the TV airwaves of this great nation how he wants to thank his Lord and Savior Jesus Christ for helping him pummel Chubby Mexican Dude's face repeatedly for four rounds with his fists. You just know he has practiced that moment over and over in front of the mirror.

Now, here comes the good part.

The Packer had just won his fourth fight. Good for him, you say. Not so good when you consider he has lost thirty-seven, including being knocked out in twenty-one of those. He does have two draws, and oh yeah, of his four wins, did I mention that two of those victories have come at the expense of Chubby Mexican Dude and his agreeable punching-bag mug? Chubby Mexican Dude currently sports a four-win and twenty-six-loss career.

But on this night, none of that matters ...the Packer is hearing the cheers.

Thought-provoking questions are now being volleyed about, and suddenly the Packer found himself having to now contemplate his boxing future ...his goals, his direction, if you will. Let's face it, he's riding the crest of a one-fight winning streak, and when momentum is on your side, you gotta keep plugging ...it's the ol' "strike while it's hot" theory. Also, keep in mind that for one of the few times in his career, the questions being lobbied in his direction have nothing to do with "where are you?" and "what day is this?"

His response to his future in the squared circle? If you're not sitting down right now, I'll pause to give you the necessary time. Trust me, this is going to get good.

OK, here we go. The Packer proceeds to announce to the entire world —well, those who happened to be ringside or had access to cable—that he wanted a shot at every single guy who had ever beaten him.

Now, stop the presses and hold everything. Think about what he just said—let it soak in—and for arguments' sake, let's just say this could possibly be arranged. We're talking about a new fight every month for the next three years, and that's only if we're talking about the beatings he took in the ring ...forget about those various beat downs at the corner bar, that incident at the grocery store, and of course, that lady at the DMV. We may have to change his name to the Paybacker.

Anyway, I say you go for it, Mr. The Packer.

Now, let's cut back to the picture I described earlier. This dog's past—his defeats if you will—mean nothing ...absolutely nothing. As I looked at him, you could just tell he was on top of the world. Our little dog was having his place in the sun, his moment, right then and there ...and in his case, just like the Packer, he got to hear the cheers of the crowd and the outpouring of appreciation. Simply put, he mattered, and on this night, so did the Packer. Forget all about the thirty-seven beatings—at that very moment they mean nothing, tonight he was the best in the world. Truth is, we all matter, even Chubby Mexican Dude.

You see, you may never get to stroll down crowded streets to an outpouring of cheers, or you may never get to punch Chubby Mexican Dude's face for four rounds ...but you matter. There are times in our life that we get a moment-oh sure, it may be an extremely small one, and no one else may know about it—but you will see, and you will be shown that you matter.

Soak it in when it happens.

Now, somebody look up Chubby Mexican Dude and give him a hug, and I mean ASAP.

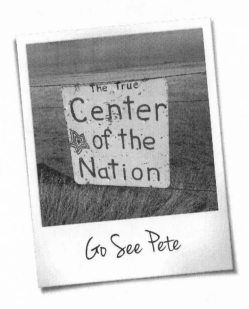

The True Center of the Nation

Go See Pete

Unlike a great many folks in my particular demographic, I am not a huge John Wayne fan.

Whoa, whoa, whoa.

Now, before you get ready to slam me into a corner or label me as one of those liberal, flag-burning, anti-establishment, gun-control-believing, un-American types ...please realize I didn't say I didn't like the man. Actually, I love John Wayne and all he stood for. Heck, I've visited Mount Rushmore, and as far as I'm concerned, there's room up there to add his chiseled mug (and while you're at it, toss Ronald Reagan up there too).

I'm just not an expert on his movies and truthfully have seen only a few in my lifetime.

I said all of that just so you would understand the significance of the following statement ...until recently, I had never heard of Belle Fourche, South Dakota. Belle as in *bell* and Fourche as in rhymes with, oh I don't know ...let's go with *goosh*.

Sturgis, South Dakota ...now, I've heard of that. Motorcycles, leather, more motorcycles, biker chicks, and finally, more motorcycles. That's my part of the world, my friend.

OK, you got me ...maybe I overstated that.

Truth is, I'd probably wreck that motorcycle before I ever got out of the parking lot. Biker chicks scare me, always have. Leather garments? OK on the jacket, but I just feel those pants would possibly give me a rash. I do look good in a do-rag, though.

Now, me and a couple of my buddies, Randy and Larry, recently found ourselves in Sturgis, South Dakota ...yet another stopping point on our road trip to Sheridan, Wyoming. We came a-whoopin' and a-hollerin' into town to check out the sights and experience some more of the beauty and unique people that make the US of A the absolute best country in the entire history of the world.

We immediately sought out the motorcycle museum and then headed over to the Harley dealership for some take-home trinkets. It was during this stop that Randy inquired if there happened to be anyone in the area who could reshape a felt cowboy hat. We had been searching for this particular person with this particular set of skills since our departure from Chickamauga several days before.

"You need to go see Pete, in Belle Fourche," the guy confidently told us. Thanking him, we paid for our merchandise and headed out to the truck ...that's when Randy turned to Larry with a smile.

"Belle Fourche!" he stated with a slight hint of old west swagger.

Larry looked at him with equal confidence, knowing exactly what he meant. It was as if they were suddenly ready to grab the reins and hop up on their trusty Palominos for the journey across the prairie that surely awaited us.

As for me, I'm in the back of the truck, munching on some M&Ms and trying to figure what a Fourche was, how you spelled it, and why it needed a bell.

Come to find out, Belle Fourche was the final destination of John Wayne's cattle drive in that classic movie *The Cowboys* ...a movie that Randy and Larry were quite familiar with and could freely quote various lines from.

We then excitedly embarked on the thirty-mile trek from Sturgis over to Belle Fourche. Thankfully we didn't cross paths with any rustlers on our way, and soon we found ourselves sliding safely into that picturesque little town and right up to the back door of Pete's Clothing & Western Wear, an oddly shaped triangular building, right there on State Street.

As we entered the store, it was very easy to pick out Pete—he was the tall, slender fellow in the Wranglers, starched shirt, Carolina blue sports coat, and a Stetson. Randy strolled over to him and truthfully; I didn't feel any type of corporately trained customer service immediately forthcoming. Pete was a stern, no-bull kind of guy; thus Larry and I took him on as a personal challenge.

Randy handed him his hat, which was badly in need of reshaping, while we inspected the premises. Now keep in mind,

Randy was a big-time rodeo dude in his day, and this hat at one time was extremely nice, however, it had spent a good twenty years up in the attic, and, well, it was in need of some major adjustment.

Pete was far from impressed; in fact, he seemed to somewhat scold Randy about the disrepair the hat had reached. He also was feeling less than confident he could do anything to rescue it and return the hat to its previous glory. That's when Larry got to cutting up, and I noticed a picture of Pete on the wall with a couple of beauty queen contestants from years back and made a few comments. We were working him as he inspected the hat further.

Pete didn't break a grin. Truthfully, I felt the slight view of a poker face; yea I've watched those guys on ESPN. He was possibly bluffing us ...after all, this is Pete arguably one of the finest hat fixers in the entire west. If he couldn't fix this hat, perhaps it simply couldn't be fixed. But, I just couldn't get a good read on him. I guess it's the southern good ol' boy in me. Shooting of the bull is what we do and someone who seems to rebuff our bull-shooting offer confuses us at times.

Finally, seemingly annoyed, he told us to go grab a bite down the street, and he'd see what he could do. We walked on down to the Stadium Sports Grill there on Fifth Avenue to grab a burger and as for me; I was somewhat puzzled that Pete had not been won over to our side mere seconds after our appearance through his back door.

We walked into the grill, and found us a table there close to the bar. It was a Saturday, an unbelievably windy and cold

Saturday and it was also college football season. Thankfully, they had a TV turned to the right channel ...it wasn't the SEC, but that was OK. Truthfully, college football means a little more in our neck of the woods than it does there in the middle of South Dakota.

The waiter came to take our order, and it was at this time that our story took an unexpected turn.

"What does this mean, Belle Fourche, South Dakota, the center of the United States?" Larry offered inquisitively as he pointed to the statement, which was proudly displayed on the back of the menu.

The waiter proceeded to tell us that as the story goes, a team of geography guys from the National Geodetic Survey performed a rather unique survey shortly after Hawaii came into the union in 1959. In essence, these fellows pulled an imaginary string from the farthest corner of Maine all the way to the farthest part of Hawaii and then pulled another equally imaginary string from the farthest part of Alaska all the way to Key West. Where those two imaginary strings crisscrossed, well, that, my friends, was the absolute center of the nation, and for the record, it was indeed Belle Fourche, South Dakota.

He left to turn our order in, while we sat in absolute dumb-founded silence. I must state, we were, as they say, somewhat in awe. This was possibly too much for us to take in at once. Here we have Pete, obviously the finest hat-fixer in these western states attempting to perform possible hat shaping magic back at the store, we're about to munch on a burger in downtown Belle Fourche, and it's all taking place at what we have just discovered is the absolute center of these United States. Yep, this is going to take a little while to digest and fully comprehend.

If only John Wayne had bellied up to the table to tell us about his latest cattle drive.

Soon our plates were placed before us. It was at this time that Larry, ever the inquisitive one, felt the need to dig just a little deeper ...*inquisite* more if you will. I'm sure inquisite is not a word, but it should be.

"You mean right where we're sitting is the absolute the center of the United States?"

Almost flippantly, our waiter guy proceeded to tell us that technically the exact point was about twenty miles north of town. "As you head north, look for old Highway 85 on your left; there'll be a little sign. Take that old dirt road for three or four miles, and you'll come up on an old metal handmade sign on your right pointing you out into a guy's field toward a monument. That spot, sitting out in the middle of this guy's pasture, is the absolute true center of the nation." Supposedly, he doesn't mind if you go take a look.

Think about it—our waiter has one of the, as far as I'm concerned; Seven Wonders of the World basically in his backyard, and it was no big deal to him. Now, get this, upon further discussion, we found he had never actually been there, and according to him, a great many folks around these parts didn't even know there was an actual spot!

We each sat there once again in total silence for a while, just eating our burgers. No one had to make a suggestion as to what our next step would be ...we just instinctively knew.

We were in that special Lewis-and-Clark zone that we get into sometimes ...it's magic to watch from afar, I am most assured.

Looks like we're going to go find us the absolute middle of this great land of ours.

We paid for our meal and headed back to Pete's for our next surprise of the day.

We walked in the back door, and Pete looked our way, but with a slight grin this time ...yep, he was suddenly on our team now. He was actually glad to see us. He walks over and presents Randy with his hat. Randy took a gander, and it was Christmas morning all over again ...yep, a true knock-me-over-with-a-feather moment. Luckily, Larry was standing close by to keep him from falling over into the finely stacked, pearl-snapped western shirts. In that short period of time, Pete had worked his magic, transforming a hat left to its lonesome all those years into perhaps the best-looking cowboy hat in the entire state of South Dakota—heck, throw the North one in too. It looked better than brand-new. I want you to know something; Pete is a craftsman, an artist if you will, and that day he became our very best friend in the entire town of Belle Fourche, South Dakota.

We took pictures with him, shot the bull with our new best bud, and then, in a most dramatic moment, we told him we had to head on out of town ...but we had one more stop to make before we shook off the dust of Belle Fourche.

Pete understood our need for adventure, and with tears in his eyes, he shook our hands and waved good-bye. Unless I'm mistaken, he and Larry shared an emotional hug. We promised the next time we moseyed on through that part of the Wild West, we would pay him a visit. (OK, maybe the tears were just a little too much dramatic effect. Let me go ahead and cut that music off too.)

We hopped back into the truck and moved onward to seek the treasure.

Now, I drove this part of the leg ...basically a typical long stretch of prairie with little to no curves to accentuate the journey. After several miles, I spotted something over to the left as we passed by. With no traffic in any direction, I simply stopped the truck right in the middle of the road, and we backed up a hundred feet or so. There it was planted in the ground over to the left of the road. A very old and very small, worn-out, hand-painted, weather-beaten, wooden sign ...a sign that simply stated *Old Highway 85*.

We turned onto the dirt road—dang, how I love a dirt road. It was a beautiful drive over several miles with a few twists and turns tossed in. Then finally, we spotted something on our right ...a bullet-ridden, hand-painted metal sign that simply read: The True Center of the Nation.

The sign was tied to four separate strands of barbwire fencing, the final strand being around forty inches off the ground. Now, my inseam at thirty-two inches was the shortest of the three of us, and I was already imagining horror stories as we approached to make this all-important leap. About three hundred feet from the fence line, out there in the field, stood an American flag that, with the strong South Dakota winds that day, resembled that iconic shot of the first flag planted on the moon.

Larry and his six-foot, five-inch frame made the step over into the pasture with somewhat ease; Randy, with his six-foot, five-inch frame was soon over as well. My turn was next, with my six-foot, one-and-three-quarter-inch frame. I slowly stepped one leg over, carefully pushing down with as much force as I could with my hands on that top strand of barbwire. I then pulled my other leg safely over ...that was a huge, applause-worthy moment.

We made our way out toward the flag, dodging cactus and cow pies, and finally, there we were, standing at this simple monument at this, the absolute center of the entire nation. The flag sat on a small concrete pad, and at the bottom of the flag was a medallion, maybe five inches across that stated the significance of that very spot.

We took pictures and basically just soaked the moment in. It is such an awesome feeling to be a true pioneer. We had accomplished something that a mere couple of hours ago, we didn't even know was accomplishable, and on a related footnote, I've never used *accomplishable* in a sentence before, yet another accomplishment.

We made our way back to the truck knowing that perhaps a ticker-tape parade awaited us back home or maybe some sort of presidential proclamation for our heroic deeds.

It was now that the final part of this story takes a somewhat tragic twist.

We repeated our most careful straddling of the barbwire fence, and again I was the last one to make the crossing. Truth be told, Randy and Larry could cross it much like Andre the Giant stepping over the top rope just before he laid a beating on the poor, soon-to-be victim on the other side of the ring.

Carefully, I raised my right leg and hoisted it slowly across that top strand, once again pushing down with all my might on the fencing. Then, I slowly began to bring my left leg over. As I crossed ever so slightly over the midway point, it became apparent that I had somehow snagged myself, and then it soon became very apparent that not only did I snag myself, but I was hooked, much like a catfish on a trotline.

Here I found myself in this most unenviable predicament for several seconds, giving me precious time to ponder my situation. I soon came to the realization that having the absolute center of one's world, if you will, perilously snagged at the absolute center of the nation is somewhat of an irony.

When I determined that no part of me was caught in this trap, only my jeans, I simply decided to go for it. I gave a mighty jerk, falling completely to the ground and ripping a hole in a very important area of said jeans. The aforementioned South Dakota winds were now reaching me in a most unusual place, but surprisingly, I was OK with it ...in fact, I found it somewhat refreshing.

Always remember this: a good road trip is not fully planned, and you must remain flexible and willing to go for it at times. Take those unexpected side journeys ...that's where the real memories sometimes await you. One more thing, if you're ever in Belle Fourche, South Dakota, drop by to see Pete. Don't let him fool ya, he's a softie.

Yep, I think it's time to go watch *The Cowboys* ...I'm feeling a John Wayne mood coming on about right now.

Given One

There are times in life that I truly feel you are "given one" ...a drop down from the heavens, a message, a sign, an event that is just for you. No one else can truly understand it ...because it's yours, it simply wasn't meant for them. Oftentimes, it cannot rationally be explained, therefore we toss around the word coincidence. In my opinion, this can occur regardless of religious affiliation or lack thereof. Atheists, agnostics...you're all fair game if you just open your eyes and pay attention from time to time.

> gi·vən wən : that which brings peace and comfort
> to you and possibly you alone...it's a specific-timing
> thing.

Sure, it's my opinion, but truthfully, I will smile at you and politely snicker with your doubts of their existence.

You see, I have seen this oftentimes-strange phenomenon occur more than once in my lifetime. Oh, I'm sure I've missed several others over the years ...I just simply wasn't paying attention. I spend so much of my life doing that. I've got to do better.

I lost my mom and dad within a couple of years of each other back in the mid-nineties. Obviously the holiday season sometimes intensifies the hurt and the missing, and yes, I am fully aware that's only natural. Most everyone my age by now has experienced that deep loss of a parent, spouse, or a child, and the holidays only serve to bring back those memories and that longing for what used to be. I used to distance myself and basically wallow in it. I know that's wrong and not healthy ...I didn't need Dr. Phil to tell me that. I promise I'm much better now though.

We all deal with things differently.

Dad has been on my mind more than normal lately. I can't explain it ...I guess it still goes back to that whole unfinished business thing; maybe it's just the season ...who knows what triggers these things. I remember Christmas with him ...helping him hunt for those special presents for mom, listening to him needle her or give her a sweet pinch just to harass her as she was cooking up festive dishes that would totally engulf our home with love and the spices of the season. Homemade dressing, fogged-up kitchen windows, and mom good-naturedly yelling "Quit it!" I can see it and I can hear it, and I'm telling you, I can almost smell it right now, I promise you I can.

My dad loved Christmas more than about any man I have ever known. I can remember sometimes hearing him giggle just like a little school kid opening presents.

Now, starting back in the late seventies, he would take a big truck down to the meat processor in Trenton and have it totally filled up to overflowing with hams. He would then start hand-delivering them to clients, associates, and friends. Not just the head of the company, but everyone he came into contact with. Eventually, I would help out ...the job was just simply getting too big for one. I'm talking a couple hundred hams.

Those hams, those ten to fifteen-pound packages of goodness and love, the memories of making those deliveries and passing them out like a stick of gum to most everyone I would meet ...Oh, I still remember those days. He gave me very few specific instructions other than "make sure you find Ms. Lane." To this day, Ms. Lane remains one of the sweetest elderly ladies I ever had the privilege of knowing. She was an extremely petite woman who always walked the sidewalks into the town of Rossville for her various errands. She did this well into her eighties. A few times she received a ride back to her home from a man named Sonny, who always drove a Chevy pickup truck and loved country music, his family, politics, and the Georgia Bulldogs. Yep, dad made sure she received one of those gold foil-wrapped pork delicacies each and every holiday season.

He was a good man with a heart as big as I want mine to be.

Every person carves his spot
and fills the hole with light.
And I pray someday I might
light as bright as he.

The other day I was being bounced around a crowded Apple Store in Nashville, shoulder to shoulder with other Apple devotees, of which I have been since 1986, thank you. As I lowered my head to plow my way to the iPad Minis, I spotted a fellow near the laptops ...dark-haired, dark-clothed ...he somehow stood out to me. I knew this guy, where had I seen him before? Just as I faked out an elderly gentleman and was sliding past a dude with tattoos surrounding his entire neck, it hit me ...Gary Burr.

Now, I don't expect you to know him. He's a songwriter ...a songwriter of the highest order in Nashville. A card-carrying member of the Songwriters Hall of Fame. I first learned of him a good fifteen years ago, shortly after my father's death. I would venture up to the Bluebird from time to time, and I know I saw him perform in the round at least once, maybe twice. Then, a few years later, I would see him often on the *Live from the Bluebird* show on cable. I remember he was very funny and could write and deliver a great song. He also used to be in a little band called Pure Prairie League back in the day for all you rock historians.

"Love's Been a Little Bit Hard On Me" ..."I Try to Think About Elvis," ...he's written tons of songs recorded by a long list of a who's who in Music City.

Now, most anytime I go to Nashville I see someone ...you know, a star. In fact, I ran into Jim Ed Brown at the Titans game the next night and had a nice conversation with him. He loved my way-cool Titans Santa hat, by the way. I never ask for an autograph or a picture during a chance meeting; I've found it best to just simply acknowledge these folks and offer a kind word and then be on my way. It's kind of like they're not on the clock if you meet them out and about. My chance meeting with Gary Burr would be no different. I acknowledged who he was, and he seemed to be a very nice and gracious guy. We exchanged pleasantries and went about our business.

I eventually made my way out to a bench in the mall. I sat there in deep thought for just a minute or so and then decided to text my son to let him know about my chance encounter with greatness. Upon receipt, he immediately texted me right back with this message:

"He wrote 'That's My Job' by Conway Twitty!"

He knew how much I loved that song, and for some strange reason, I simply had no idea that Gary Burr had written it. In case you've never heard of it, it tells the story of a son and his relationship with his dad from childhood, the tension of those teen years, and later, adulthood and all its complications. Finally after his father's death, the son realizes that it is now his job to go on, because "everything I do is because of you." By going on with his life, he's keeping his dad "safe with me." Trust me when I say this is a song that will tear up the hardest heart of the burliest of men, especially the way Conway could bring it. In fact, I rank it right up there with "Make Believe" as the two greatest Conway songs of all-time. ("Hello Darling," you get the bronze.)

I began to think back on the words and their meaning as I sat there, I'm sure at times with my eyes closed, trying to recreate the song in my mind. I desperately needed to hear it again. Then, through the magic of satellites and cell towers and computer technology and Steve Jobs, I was able to watch Conway belt it out right then and there on my phone.

It was even better than I remembered.

Now, to you, that perhaps is not that big of a deal, and I can understand that ...but, it wasn't meant for you. It was my gift. This simple chance meeting with a songwriting hero of mine, leading to the discovery that he had written a song that has and continues to affect me so. A song that spoke to me at just the right time.

Great songs will do that.

And he said "That's my job
that's what I do.
Everything I do is because of you
to keep you safe with me.
That's my job, you see."
"That's My Job" by Gary Burr

I suddenly felt like a freshly bathed baby, wrapped up in absolute peace, as I sat on that bench for the longest, watching stressed-out Christmas shoppers pass by. I had a reassurance if you will. I could hear the holiday music and seemingly almost smell those hams.

It was as if Dad had passed by.

Yep, as far as I'm concerned, I was given one the other day at the Green Hills Mall in Nashville, Tennessee, and thankfully, I was paying attention.

This holiday season, I hope you're given one too.

Thank you, Gary Burr, thank you, Conway, and thank you, Daddy ...Merry Christmas.

A Great American

It would have been around 1977 or so ...yep, around that time that I first heard mention of Lewis Grizzard. This would have been shortly after he had returned to the *Atlanta Constitution* after spending his last miserable winter in Chicago. Lewis was a sports columnist then, seemingly such a meaningless title for a man of his talents ...much like giving Hemingway the political beat at the county courthouse. I guess we all need titles.

A few years later, I can remember specifically reading an article that Lewis had written about funerals in the south. An article that was affixed to a Kenmore refrigerator with a magnet at a buddy's house. An article that I read twice before I actually reached inside for a cold beverage.

Now, there's a Marriott on the left hand side just past Marietta as you head south on I-75 and just before you actually find yourself in the heart of Atlanta. I once found myself in a rather large meeting room there along with about fifteen other folks ...had to be around 1985. We were discussing various pie charts and graphs and dissecting market research and focus group findings, all the while trying to out-do each other with our vast knowledge of the latest marketing acronyms straight from Madison Avenue. CPP, CPM, POP, LTO, BOGO ...speakers would toss them around to give their speeches more validity. At times, it seemed almost like we spoke in code. After an absolutely lovely morning, it was announced that food would be brought to us at the lunch hour, and we were also told that a guest would be joining us. I'm thinking another marketing dude with a whole new bunch of acronyms. I found myself approaching a state of giddy, or SOG for all you marketing whizzes, as the noon hour approached us.

Soon, white-clad waiters were bringing china plates to our table, and we began to munch on our selection of greens with that special house dressing and the whitest piece of chicken you ever saw. Suddenly, the door opened up, and in sashayed a lanky gentleman wearing a white golf shirt, khakis, I'm thinking possibly Gucci loafers with no socks, an Augusta green sport coat, and a smirk that I later determined he carried with him most everywhere he went. Mr. Lewis Grizzard ...how do you do.

I can't remember what I had for supper last night, and if you were to ask me what I am wearing right now I would have to look first to tell you, but somehow I remember the details of this particular event. I find that strange. No, I do not recall a bit of what he said, but I do remember laughing frequently.

I also recall knowing specifically at that very moment that *this* was a moment. Moments occur more often than we realize, and they are rarely created ...as stated, they simply occur.

I so wish we had camera phones and Facebook, and the Internet and texting and a whole slew of other intra-web thingies back then ...things that I'm quite sure Lewis would have detested even to this day. I would not only have been able to document my youth and chiseled features but also immortalize the very day that I met one of the finest southern writers of the last half of the twentieth century.

I met him, I shook his hand, and for goodness' sake, I even had a somewhat lengthy conversation with a true American icon. I was very aware at the time of whom I was in the presence of, unlike others in that room that I just don't think really got it. These other folks were Yankees—bless their hearts—who most assuredly had made their move south to grace us with their obvious superior intellect. Why folks equate our accent with a lack of gray matter baffles me at times. Another subject for another day.

I will not attempt to write a biography of Mr. Grizzard; it's already been done numerous times by folks far better at crafting descriptives from a keyboard than myself. I will say this however ...a man that so deeply loved his mama, dogs, small towns, the South, Elvis, the Georgia Bulldogs, and the magic of the written word would have been sent to the very top of my buddy list posthaste if given such the chance.

He was politically incorrect before we had really coined that phrase. He detested fishing, computers, TV evangelists, and a few other things that I won't mention to prevent further controversy. It seemed, at times, that he simply did not possess an inner monologue, and he would absolutely, without fear, put his thoughts on paper for everyone to read.

That day would most certainly have made the highlight reel of my life.

Just a few years ago, I found myself in action-packed Pigeon Forge. I was bored and sitting on a bench at an outlet mall eating a funnel cake and trying to figure out something to prevent me from not only falling asleep but also give out the impression that I was indeed having the time of my life, and this truly was the Champs-Elysées of East Tennessee. I decided to find a book, perhaps a Lewis Grizzard gem that I had not yet read.

I entered Grizzard into Google on my newly acquired iPhone. I can recall realizing that adding "Lewis" to the search would obviously not be necessary. All kinds of stuff started popping up including curiously an eBay listing ...a link that I selected with much interest. This link took me to a listing for a large, framed copy of the famous Mike Luckovich editorial cartoon that ran in the *Atlanta Constitution* on March 22, 1994 ...two days after Lewis Grizzard had "up and died" in an Atlanta hospital. The cartoon showed Lewis approaching the pearly gates, book in hand, and his beloved black lab, Catfish, excitedly running out to meet him. Catfish had passed away just a few months before. This, my friend, was truly a priceless American treasure.

I simply had to have this cartoon ...ironically, a cartoon that a lady no more than forty-five minutes south of my house had placed on the open market. I immediately sent an e-mail, and later that day, I would find that this seemingly priceless gem was still in her possession.

Today, I am most proud to say that this cartoon, this much-coveted collectible in my eyes, prominently hangs within arm's reach of the computer keyboard in my office.

Lewis's paths and mine had indeed crossed one more time.

Today, there's a tombstone in a small cemetery in Moreland, Georgia, that simply states "A Great American."

Yes, he most certainly was.

Old Glory Hangs
off Old Bethel

Head just south out of Chickamauga, down toward the cove ...
then hang a left onto Old Bethel. Now, drive just a bit, maybe
a half a mile ...then take a gaze to your right, out toward the
woods.

There she hangs.

I stumbled upon this lovely sight just the other day, and it
kind of startled me at first. Kind of the same feeling I got the
very first time I saw the Goodyear Blimp flying overhead. It's a
feeling of awe, surprise, and just flat-out childlike astonishment
all rolled into one.

I drove for just a couple hundred feet down a dirt road to
get a better look. Got out of the Jeep, took a few pictures, and
just stood there and soaked it in. This was a huge flag ...I'm
thinking maybe thirty-five to forty feet tall. It's quite impressive

to see it hanging from the trees out there all to itself. I know the fellow who hung it, and he did a mighty fine job.

I was about to head on out when it hit me to take a look at it again ...but this time, walk out into the woods and look back at it, you know, from the other side. In other words, look at it from a different perspective.

I walked across the dirt road, headed out into the woods, and found me a good spot. I turned around for this new look at Old Glory, and, yes, I guess you could say that our flag was still there.

Now, I've seen the Statue of Liberty, I've seen the White House, I've seen the Grand Canyon, I've seen countless other monuments and pieces of America that stir the soul, but this old, tattered flag hanging from the trees out in the woods stood shoulder to shoulder with them all at that particular moment. I simply stood there and watched the sun beaming over Lookout Mountain and tossing its rays through the worn, faded fabric ... my gosh, how could you not be moved.

I'm thinking about that moment right now as the presidential race heats up. I'm thinking of it as I see the latest political ads and excerpts from various convention speeches splashed across the multiple news outlets we have at our disposal. I'm sorry to say that I have become so very cynical with the whole political process over the years, at both the local and national level. I simply do not believe that one party and one party alone is to blame for whatever ails our country right now. I totally despise this whole blame-shifting game, and frankly, it offends me that someone feels I am naïve enough to believe their well-rehearsed, poll-driven diatribes that carry simple messages of just what the followers want to hear ...their own opinions spoken right back to them. Speeches crafted to offend as few as possible, shift all the blame, and provide the grayest of answers to the issues of the day.

Simply put, the older I get, the more I realize this one undeniable fact: no one is totally wrong, and no one is totally right.

Age and I guess you would say experience have taught me that.

When you feel you have all the right answers and are not willing to listen to another opinion or at least try to see things from the other man's perspective, I tend to tune you out as well. That goes for both sides ...be it liberal/conservative, Democrat/Republican, or whatever labels you want to use. I truly feel our system is not Good Guys vs. Bad Guys.

Yes, I have some strong opinions and views. I have softened on some, and, yes, on some I've even changed my opinion over the years.

Age has shown me some things as well.

I hear talk of the way things "used to be" ...you know, the so-called good old days and how we have strayed from the values that once made this country great. In part, I can most certainly agree with that statement, although I would argue with anyone that we are still the greatest country on this planet. However, before you yearn too strongly for those so-called good old days, why not ask an elderly African American friend of mine who lives just a few miles from me about those good old days ...perhaps you will be exposed to a somewhat different perspective.

Those days weren't necessarily good for all.

You see, just like that flag hanging out in the woods, there are two sides, and you need to look at both of them to get the full picture ...that goes for whichever side of the flag you presently stand on.

O say, if we could just see.

More Decembers to See

I returned home yesterday afternoon from another funeral. Yes, this activity has become a part of my life more with each and every passing of December. The days steadily proceed and eventually all of us, at varying times, simply will not be able to keep up. I know this, but I do not *want* to know this.

It was shocking in that I had just seen him a week before he died and we had exchanged pleasantries, as they say. Why do I mention this? I realize it is rather odd when I think about it. It's as though, in my mind, since I had just seen him, he was still a part of my life and thus, he should continue to be. He simply was not supposed to die yet.

He was the brother of one of my best friends. He was a quiet man whom I had known since childhood. No, we were not close ...but close enough to feel the sting and also hurt for my buddy.

Fifty-five. At one time in my life, I would have found this to be just about right ...as if death naturally comes after a certain age. As my years keep passing, I have come to realize that this wasn't right ...in my mind he had many more Decembers to see.

He was a good man. We seem to never have enough of those and I just hate to see another one go.

Just before bedtime, I was reflecting on the day. Funeral services always tend to bring out those periods of self-analysis and this one was no different. Then, I received the news. News that I could not grasp at first, I had to just stop, stop everything and absorb it. It was as if I had to breathe deeply several times before I could simply move or begin to put words together to announce what I had just learned. I had lost yet another friend. Yes, a very special one.

I can close my eyes and still see her playing with all of us other kids at the community pool where we grew up. Cheering at our football games. Running around the gym during P.E. Club. She was a prankster and although she was a very pretty girl, she was like having another buddy in the group. I so loved her for that.

I ran into her mother a few years back at a wedding here in town and she told me that my friend had re-married and was living over in the Carolinas ...the South one to be exact.

I sent an email to her several days later and soon we were able to start catching up. We would exchange verbal missiles and I could tell she was still that same feisty girl from our school days. Over the years, we would check in on each other from time to time. She was so happy and she was at peace and had found a wonderful husband. She was still very outgoing, but in parts of her life she was a very private person. She joined the masses on Facebook, but she didn't use her name, just a self-appointed moniker. She would let you in, but not totally into her life.

Truthfully, she was fighting cancer and it became apparent to me that she simply did not want to talk about. The constant requests for latest news and thinly disguised prognosis updates ...she wanted no part of that. Yes, cancer was part of her life and had been for several years, but she refused to make it her life. She had other things to do and although she was very aware of her situation and finally, her prognosis, it was as if she refused to participate. In our emails over the years, we simply never discussed it. Every so often she would post some sort of treatment update, or possibly a latest update on news from the doctor on her Facebook account and sometimes I would reply. Somehow, she had a way of making the worst news seem upbeat at times. Life and death ...she seemingly laughed at both.

She came through town five or six years ago and we were able to meet at my office and talk and yes, we both could do that very well. We spent the afternoon, just two old friends, who still, in some ways, knew each other better than friends we would see on a weekly basis. Childhood friends can be that way sometimes.

I will miss her, not because she was a part of my daily life, but because she was the dearest of friends. Those rare and very special friends who serve as a reminder of the way things used to be. In an odd way, as long as she was there, those days were still there too. I will still revisit those days, simply go back in my mind from time to time and I'm sure she will always be waiting to see me with a wisecrack and a laugh.

I have never met her daughter, a daughter who married just three months ago. I saw the pictures and she has her mother's eyes and smile. If she has just a small portion of her mother's grace, she will always light up most any room she ever enters and will leave those disappointed when it is time for her to leave. I want to meet her someday and tell her that.

Yep, she was too young, but nowadays, it seems they all are. To be honest, that age when appropriate departure from this earth is fitting and just, I simply do not know. I do know this, it just doesn't seem it should be fifty-two.

So, this morning, I'm thinking about two families who are hurting. I'm thinking about two people who are now gone from my life and I simply have to realize that He had determined they had each seen all of their Decembers.

Death is nothing at all,
I have only slipped into the next room
I am I and you are you
Whatever we were to each other, that we are still.

My belief is His plan is perfect and today, so are they.

Left It All at the Track

I went to my very first NASCAR race last night, and here are some of my observations.

First of all, I cheered for Kurt Busch all night long, mainly because he's an outlaw, just like me. Now, with that in mind, imagine my horror this morning when I woke up and jumped on the ol' NASCAR website only to find that the #18 car I cheered for all night long belonged to his brother, Kyle. Kurt was in the #51 car, a car to which I paid little or no attention to the entire night.

Kurt Busch—he's the one who dog-cussed that reporter a month or so ago for asking some lame question. Let's face it; he's tired of dealing with the public. Actually, he and his brother are both like the bad guys in pro wrestling. You need guys like that to make things interesting. Go ahead and toss Tony Stewart in there too; you gotta love a guy who will throw his helmet at a guy's car ...I mean, who does that? Sometimes I guess I just love the guys who wear the ol' black helmet ...you know, the ones that spit at old ladies, won't hold your baby for a picture, and of course, blow off those pesky reporters.

Let's face it, who would want to see a whole track full of Jeff Gordons being all polite and exchanging in-race pleasantries? Five bucks says Gordon has a Pinterest account.

Mark Martin, that's another story. I was told by a good buddy, who shall remain nameless, that since I know absolutely nothing about NASCAR that maybe I should pull for Mark Martin. Spurdog (sorry, I let that slip) said that everybody loves Mark Martin because he's so old. He's kind of like the grandfather to all the other drivers. There are constant jokes about his age: he never turns his blinker off, he drives extra-slow in the fast lane, he's the only guy on the track driving a four-door. People are constantly amazed that he can even find the track, much less actually drive on it. I'm loving it. "Let's cheer for that old geezer!" I said with a mocking laugh. So, once again, imagine my horror and dismay when I check out his bio this morning to find that I am two—yep, that's right—two days older than the Larry King of the NASCAR set. I immediately got off the computer after that one.

Yes, I saw a bunch of drunken rednecks, but no more than any other sporting event I've ever attended. Yes, I did see much more skin from a few ladies than I should. In fact, I saw parts of some "ladies" that I'm not supposed to see unless I pay for such a privilege. But let's face it, I go to Wal-Mart a couple of times a month ...it's gonna take more than granny wearing an extra-small Earnhardt Jr. tank top trying to cover up at least a triple-X area to truly shock me anymore.

All in all, I had a great time. Hung out with some great buddies—Rocky, Jimmy, David, Spencer, Spurdog, Brian—and made a few new ones ...Dan, you're the man. I also found out that my buddy Brian is not only a great friend, but also an absolute walking encyclopedia on the sport. I also learned to appreciate the fact that NASCAR is much more than just making left-hand turns all night. It takes athletic ability and guts to drive those cars at that kind of speed.

Seriously, put me behind the wheel, and I can't get from Monteagle to the Winchester exit without a nature-call pit stop and another Diet Mountain Dew. Those guys control all bodily functions and Little Debbie cravings for like five hundred miles. I do think it would be interesting to put up a Cracker Barrel billboard, say in turn three, and see if that messes with their concentration level any. Or, how about a flashing Krispy Kreme "Hot Now" sign as you pull into pit row? That might make things just a little more compelling as well.

Also, on a side note, I sat on those aluminum bleachers for over four hours. That includes pre-race warm-ups, introductions, thank-yous, and photo-ops for representatives from just about every marketable product in this great country of ours, as well as an entire Montgomery Gentry concert. The pain in my lower extremities was reaching medical attention stage, and they hadn't even dropped the flag yet. Trust me on this one, the throbbing in my hindquarters at times was simply beyond comprehension; I nearly blacked out once. Thanks to some advice from some of the more seasoned race-goers, I learned to lean right and left several times and was able to fight through the torment ...that and a couple of action-breaking caution flags helped immensely.

This morning I feel beat, but I'll be fine. Yep, I truly left it all at the track ...now, there's your athletic ability and guts.

You ain't got squat on me, Mark Martin.

Ducks on the Pond

My mother loved holidays.

Now, when I say holidays, I'm talking strictly about the "Big Six," and you know what they are:

1. New Year's Day
2. Valentine's Day
3. Easter
4. Halloween
5. Thanksgiving
6. Christmas

She loved them for the traditions and the memories and because it gave her a reason to cook, decorate, and otherwise transform her house into her very own reflection of the season. Of course, this would all culminate with her annual over-the-top, pre-Pinterest, "hand me some more thumb tacks, I'm never doing this again as long as I live, has anyone seen the Scotch tape?" Christmas-decorating extravaganza.

Yep, Christmas was kind of like mom's own personal decorating Olympics if you will, and the training and preparation for this annual event began months before the opening ceremonies, which were shortly after midnight on November first. She would be tossing jack-o'-lanterns and Halloween candy out the back door as I was bringing various artificial holiday decorative items though the front. It was actually a good weeklong transformation, and she always used red and green ...forget all those trendy colors. To mom's credit, she was old school when it came to the entire two-month Christmas season; however, she did branch out into those "highly sought-after" Department 56 dust catchers in her later years. I think she saw it as an investment as well; after all, look at all of those Beanie Baby millionaires out there. Mom was so good at what she did that she received several offers to turn pro, but she turned each of them down flat. She was such a purist, truly the Bobby Jones of the home decorating set.

Looking back, Thanksgiving kind of got the shaft on the decorating end. Mom would end up with this strange Pilgrim/Turkey/Santa Claus/Baby Jesus mishmash that I understood and appreciated, although I'm not quite sure what the early settlers and the Indians would have thought about it. However, one taste of her dressing and her sweet potato casserole, and I'm quite sure they would have totally bought into it and stayed not only to watch the Lions take their annual holiday beat down on our TV (which would have been in glorious Technicolor, I might add), but grab a sample of her banana pudding as well. They would each leave with not only their bellies full, but they also would carry with them a lovely aroma of rosemary, ginger, and apple-spice for weeks after they returned to their humble villages.

Truthfully, my mom was a wonderful decorator and the best cook to ever walk this planet, and I so wish she could have lived long enough to see the Food Network, HGTV, Ina Garten, Paula Deen, Pinterest, and iPads.

You just have no idea.

It's now nearing the Easter season of 1977 ...my senior year in high school. Mom has been busy decorating, and each day when I got back home from school, there would be another pastel bunny or maybe a collection of eggs to be found around the house. When I think back on it, mom made me an Easter basket every year, and yes, I know that is absolutely not an uncommon occurrence. I would receive my last Easter basket at the age of thirty-four, just a few weeks before she passed away. She never missed a year.

I so miss my baskets.

On Easter morning that year, my basket was sitting on the kitchen table as usual, but this time, mom had a surprise. She told me to go look out in the carport. When I opened the back door, I could hear quacking. There, just over to the left in a cage ...sat two baby ducks.

Now, growing up I was always getting pets. Of course, I always had a dog, but I would from time to time also make purchases at the old Grant's Department Store with allowance money I had saved up. Miniature turtles, goldfish, guinea pigs, tropical fish, hamsters with those really cool hamster tread-mills they use—you name it. I think we had possibly discussed ducks before after seeing some at the hardware store. Now, as I am nearing the end of my public school career, I found myself suddenly the proud father of two of the cutest little quackers you ever saw. I immediately named them Ralph and Herbie, and the bonding took place even quicker. Looking back, they could have been girls for all I knew. I just truly did not see the need to get that personal with them to acquire further information.

Each day when I would return home from ball practice or a game, Ralph and Herbie would be waiting on me. I would get them out of their cage, and we'd play in the yard for the longest. They would come to me like puppy dogs, and I would roll in the grass with them, lots of times still wearing my ball uniform. We became unbelievably close.

I never lost sight of the inevitable. Ralph and Herbie would not always be mine ...that wouldn't be fair to them. They would one day need a new home, the Duck Pond in Rossville, just a short drive from the house.

It was the week of my graduation, and I made the decision on my own. It was time to take my boys to their new home. Equipped with a loaf of bread, I loaded them up and was about to head out when at the last minute, my dad wanted to ride along with me. I remember being somewhat surprised; it just felt awkward. You see, my dad and I were sometimes not the best communicators ...at least with each other, and this just didn't seem like something we would do together.

We hopped into my '71 Chevy pickup, the one that used to belong to him, and made the twelve-minute drive to downtown Rossville. Just past the old Peerless Mill, we made the turn there on Andrews Street, a block from the Duck Pond. It's nearing that "magic hour" now; the sun giving all it touched that golden glow just before it shows off its wide spectrum of pink hues. I expertly coasted to a stop, releasing the clutch and break just as I turn the ignition off. I was proud of my driving skills, my smooth and proper use of the clutch, brake, gas pedal and gear shift ...driving skills I had learned in this very vehicle, from this very teacher. I hopped out and reached for Ralph and Herbie's cage that sat there in the bed, up against my toolbox. I honestly believe they were excited.

The next few moments weren't emotional ones for me as I recall. Actually, I felt a great deal of satisfaction. I had done my job very well over the last six weeks, and I had made friends now that I could drop by and see most anytime I wanted to ... after all, surely I could pick out my two ducks from the other fifty or more who called this wonderful place home.

I sat Ralph and Herbie down, patted them on the head, and they waddled the few remaining feet to the water as I sat there on the bank like a proud parent watching my boys enter their new world for the very first time. Wouldn't you know it— the old saying "like a duck takes to water" is so true.

About that time, dad sat down on the bank right beside me, along with my loaf of bread. We started slowly pinching off pieces and tossing them out to the ducks. Quickly, all of the ducks swam up near us as we offered up the delicacies. I loved watching them chase after the bread.

Then, we just began talking.

Obviously, I can't tell you what we talked about, but it just seemed to flow so easily, maybe for the first time ever. We talked, tossed bread, and talked some more.

Finally, all the bread was gone, and the ducks, including Ralph and Herbie, swam off to do duck things but we just sat there and kept right on talking. It was as if we had a lifetime to catch up on. We talked and at times we just watched the ducks until late in the night …a beautiful night, a starry night, and I knew very well at that moment, a very special night. Finally, we decided to head on back home, saying good-bye to Ralph and Herbie as they were busy making new friends.

It was well after 11:00 when we walked in the back door at the house. A house now void of any decorations …Independence Day would be coming up in a little over a month, but as we have already established, the birth of our nation did not exist on mom's festivities calendar.

A day or so later, I dropped back by the pond, and I could still pick out Ralph and Herbie, but I knew already the day would soon come when I simply wouldn't know them anymore. That was OK. I wanted them to fit in, and they looked so happy.

It's many years later now, and yes, I still drop by the Duck Pond every once in a while. I often wonder if any of those ducks swimming carefree and enjoying life have a Ralph or Herbie in their ancestral tree. I like to think some do.

Yes, a few times over the years, I have made my way over to the very spot where my father and I sat that night. I'm fortunate my mind can still go back there very easily.

I never told him what that night meant to me, and I should have, but for some reason, that's just not the way most of us guys are made.

I so hate that.

One for Roy

Growing up I held a fascination, as did most boys of my generation, with the Wild West. Roy Rogers and Gene Autry were
a big part of my Saturday morning TV viewing back in those
days, and I tended to like Roy best. This was back in the days
when the bad guys wore black hats, saloons made drinking
whiskey look like a simple little glass of iced tea, and when you
got shot, there was no blood.

What red-blooded boy wouldn't want to head out West?

The dusty prairies, where we'd hunt down no-good hom-
bres during the day, then sing songs around a campfire outside
the bunkhouse at night. Oh yeah, one more thing, we'd always
get the girl too. You just knew we would.

Two of my best friends, Randy and Big Larry, wanted to
head out West too, but they decided to leave the hunting-down-
bad-guys part to the proper law enforcement officials. Their

mission was to go elk hunting. This required months and months of preparation, arranging accommodations, coordinating travel schedules, and of course, acquiring their elk tags. After putting all the details together, they then did the unimaginable ...they asked me if I would like to tag along.

I screamed like I had just won a beauty pageant. Tears were flowing as I accepted their most gracious invitation.

Truthfully, I'm good on road trips. First of all, I love to drive; in fact, keep me supplied with Diet Mountain Dew, and I can go for extremely long distances, as long as there are nature breaks on the hour. I'm a good listener, and I also obey all traffic laws. Some would say I drive rather slowly, but I say one can never be too careful.

We left out on a Wednesday to make the cross-country trip to the Flying H Ranch in Big Horn, Wyoming. Nonstop driving time from our neck of the woods would be about twenty-four straight hours. The Flying H is a twenty-thousand-acre ranch nestled right beneath the mountains in Big Horn, just outside of Sheridan. Picture a cross between *Bonanza* and a Coors commercial, and you're getting close. To be honest, there are no totally encompassing adjectives to fully paint the picture of the scenery out there.

Again, the purpose of the trip, other than the obvious adventure and great times, was to hunt enormous bull elks. Both Larry and Randy wanted to not only shoot one of these massive animals, but also do it in the snow ...that would be the ultimate dream. However, Randy had one more purpose in mind. Randy's brother-in-law, Roy Dickson, passed away four years ago. He would have been fifty this year, and Roy had always wanted to shoot a big bull elk out West ...a dream that was never realized. Randy's quest was to do it to honor Roy, and to further honor him, he was going to do it with Roy's gun.

Now, anyone who knows me knows it's laughable to think I would go hunting, and they're right. Not only do I not know how, but also every animal I see I immediately want to name it and start talking baby talk to it. The only thing I can shoot is a camera and the bull, and I so love doing both.

So, you see, I am probably one of the only guys that you will ever meet who went on a non-hunting hunting trip. I was on an adventure with two buddies, one whom I have known since the first grade. They both are hunting, outdoor kind of guys, and I loved the way they knew all about trees and animals and guns.

We traveled for the most part on two-lane roads, which is the way God intended for man to see the world, and trust me, we saw a big chunk of it. We saw about every wild animal you could imagine ...all from the safety of a big Ford F250. One day in particular, we saw the Crazy Horse Memorial, then Mount Rushmore and Sylvan Lake, as well as some antelope, prairie dogs, mule deer, whitetail deer, coyotes, raccoons, all kinds of birds migrating, and some wild buffaloes.

I love buffaloes.

When we arrived four days later on Sunday afternoon, the skies were a deep blue and there was no snow to be found, unless you looked way up into the mountains where you could make out just a hint. The guys met up with our guides and did some practice shooting, and then we headed back to the ranch.

The aroma of something scrumptious met us at the back door. It was a feast that would have made Gabby Hayes give out a yell. The meal was prepared by Mandy, a very nice and fun lady from Wales who looked after us our entire stay. She made shepherd's pie with lamb, and I believe it was my favorite meal of the whole trip.

With our bellies full and the bull completely shot, we all retired to our bunks. We were going to be up and at 'em by six.

I woke up around four with that same kind of rush I still get each and every Christmas morning. I lay there wide awake, excited about getting out there and experiencing it all.

I finally heard the guys milling about, so I made my way out into the kitchen for some coffee ...and a surprise. During the night it had started to snow, and we could see by the moonlight that it was still coming down hard.

I gave thanks to the one who had sent it.

Soon our guides, Dan and Duffy, showed up. We drank some coffee, they all discussed strategy, and then we split up. Larry and Duffy took off to begin their tracking work, while Randy, Dan, and I headed in another direction.

We spent much of the day driving way up into the mountains, looking for markings in the area, any signs of possible movement. The snow would add another wrinkle to the hunt. For some reason, I just figured you got out of the truck, stood there for a while, spotted an elk strolling by, pulled the trigger ...big boom, elk done, game over. I soon found that it is way more involved than that. There's miles and miles of hiking, checking through the scopes, followed by hiking some more. You are truly stalking and using your knowledge of the land and your prey.

We met back up that afternoon and over dinner discussed the day. We had seen elk in the distance through scopes, and the guys were putting together a battle plan for the following day while I played with Wiener, Mandy's dachshund.

Wiener was thirteen and had a belly that he dragged slowly across the carpet as he made his rounds. I soon learned he had been to seventeen countries, actually smuggled into a few. He was kidnapped once in Moscow and held for ransom; a note demanding $2,000 was left behind. After intense negotiations, the ransom was paid, and Wiener was safely delivered back to Mandy ...an absolutely true story. He once found a mass grave of over two hundred and fifty Croatians, which had gone un-discovered for over six years ...again, absolutely true. The ru-mor around here is he did undercover work for the CIA, but Wiener simply wouldn't discuss it.

Bottom line, if James Bond had a dog, he would be a wie-ner dog named Wiener, who is retired now and living a quiet and happy life at the Flying H Ranch in Big Horn, Wyoming.

Well, it's bedtime. Good night, boys, good night, Mandy ... good night, Wiener.

The next day, we again split up early and headed out. Randy, Dan, and I had made our way far up into the moun-tains. The snow was continuing to come down. We settled under a gathering of crystal-covered trees as they looked out across a seemingly endless sea of white. It's midmorning, and we hear a shot off in the distance toward the north ...the direction where Larry and Duffy had headed. Soon we got the call—Larry had indeed taken down a bull elk.

We immediately headed toward them in snow that at times reached above the fender wells on the truck. Thankfully Dan knew these mountains well enough to know where the actual road lay.

We were within half a mile from Larry and Duffy when our luck ran out ...we were stuck, and I mean good. I jumped out to find that the snow was in places near my waist.

Now, keep in mind, I'm from the South. Around here, we close schools because a weatherman just mentioned the possibility of a flurry. Let three or four flakes stack up, and we raid the grocery stores like vultures over road kill. The milk and bread sections are wiped out first, because, well, that's just what we do. We like snow, but somehow we're scared of the stuff; the mere rumor sends us into full-on, zombie-style survival mode.

Dan made a call over to Duffy that we needed some chains.

Soon a rather large pickup truck came bouncing up the hillside, snow exploding with each meeting of the tires. Larry was on the passenger side, wearing a big grin ...a grin that he has a way of carrying with him most places.

Dan began expertly applying the chains like it was a pit stop at Daytona, while Larry, still riding his adrenaline rush, started giving us a play-by-play of his big score. Before he could really get going, the chains were on, and it was time to head over and see what all the fuss had been about.

We made our way on down a hill and then over several hundred feet, and there it was. Now, I live right next to Chickamauga Park, the largest military park in the country. Acres and acres of historical battlefields surrounded by natural beauty, and it's totally infested with deer. I have seen deer by the thousands over the years, but they were simply miniature poodles compared to this animal. A big bull elk ...seven hundred and some odd pounds of muscle, with a rack that stretched out in each direction for several feet. Larry not only had a trophy, but enough meat to feed all of Varnell at least through winter and into spring.

We helped load it up and headed back down toward the ranch. Big Larry's quest is complete.

That night we sat around and talked about the events of the day ...even Wiener seemed excited. I knew Randy was now feeling the pressure. Kind of like a pitcher sitting in the dugout; it's the bottom of the eighth, and he's working on a no-hitter. He knows he has to go back out there one more time; his teammates won't dare talk about it. Everyone is pulling for him, but it is totally up to him now. Those are some lonely and tense moments.

Early the next morning, Randy and Dan took off for the ridges behind us that we had been analyzing and scoping since we started just a few days before. Larry and I left out to ride the snow-covered roads back into the mountains with Duffy simply to look for elk and enjoy the morning.

A couple of hours had passed when we pulled up on a ridge overlooking a deep, snow-covered valley. It was then that Duffy and Larry spotted through binoculars an elk standing way off on a ridge.

Then they spotted Randy, some distance away from that elk.

Larry suddenly had the perfect spot to witness the event. In my most humble opinion, this was not merely a coincidence ...I'm telling you, it was meant to be.

I'm proud to tell you that on Wednesday morning, November 2, 2011, at 9:09 a.m., the dream and the mission were completed. Randy took down a huge 6×6 bull elk on a frigid but sunny nineteen-degree morning.

And so it was, high up in the mountains overlooking Big Horn, a tribute was paid, a dream fulfilled. It was a beautiful day ...it was a perfect day. The snow absolutely sparkled from the sun's attention, and the cloudless skies were so blue you could almost see right into heaven. If I had only looked harder, maybe I could have. I need to work on that.

Later that day, we ended up on yet another great road trip, this time to the Devil's Tower and then back into Sheridan that night for steaks.

We never quit laughing.

You know, I bet Roy was laughing too.

The Day Pug
Pulled the Rug

To say she was a very beautiful girl would be far too simplistic ...I liken it to referring to the Taj Mahal as a very nice house. There needs to be a new, all-encompassing descriptive created. I'll have to work on that.

The loveliest of birds would surround her very presence. Her feet simply never touched the ground, and the enchanting aroma of honey and lilacs, as well as all the fifth-grade boys, followed her as she floated by. She was absolute perfection in knee socks and black-and-white saddle oxfords, and I am convinced to this day that God simply doesn't make fifth-grade girls like that anymore. If He did, no red-blooded fifth-grade boy would ever want to venture into the sixth.

She was the very first girl to firmly establish in my mind that yes, girls were different, but that different is really, really good at times.

We had just moved to the neighborhood a few months before, a neighborhood full of hills and kids. I could see her house one street over and up one of those hills before the trees would bloom again in the spring. Now, for an eleven-year-old boy totally petrified of these newly discovered foreign objects, this distance may as well have been across the country. In fact, Teddy Roosevelt wouldn't have taken that journey. Not only that, but I was somewhat convinced her house was surrounded by a full-time staff of security guards equipped with assault rifles in the event a strange boy such as myself was to approach the gates. I rationalized that it was simply best for me to remain on my hill. You know, the ol' "worship from afar" scenario.

I would find myself looking her way too many times at school. Everything she did was artful, and it was as if that was the way things were supposed to be done. The way she folded her papers, sharpened her pencil, carried her books ...you name it. We made eye contact a few times, and I know that we most likely exchanged pleasantries on more than one occasion. I would have tried to give off an air of calmness on the outside while my innards resembled those girls on the Ed Sullivan show screaming, squalling, and trying not to pass out at the very sight of the Beatles.

Suddenly, baseball and football—heck, even my buddies and the Three Stooges—didn't seem quite as important as they once did.

Now, I must tell you, I had a dog back then, a mutt named Pug. If you could go on DogAncestry.com and trace his family tree back several generations, I'm sure you'd still come up with just more mutt. He was part everything. Think of a German Shepherd crossed with a Beagle, throw in some Pit Bull, and then top it off with a mashed-up front face like a Pug. He was a good ol' dog that I had brought with me from our old house in the valley. Thinking back, I believe he was my first dog. We were the best of friends and did everything together.

That is, until the incident.

I remember I was playing outside that afternoon, working on my near flawless-pitching form, the rubber baseball bouncing off the back of our house. You see, I had chalked off a strike zone onto the red brick and carefully measured the proper distance away down to the exact quarter inch. I would spend hours out there pitching and working on my control. Truth be told, I still hold all the pitching records from that backyard.

I had just finished yet another complete game shutout and was walking around the side of the house to meet with the reporters, just before I retired to the locker room, when I saw her. She was standing at the end of my driveway smiling, and honestly, I don't remember anything about the next few moments. I do remember when I came to myself; I was standing face to face with the girl from a hill and one street over. It was very my own Robert Redford/Glenn Close/*The Natural* moment if you will.

At that precise instant, Frank Capra would have cued the music, and the sun would have softly released its rosy red hue engulfing everything around us. The camera would begin pulling back, showing the dashing, young, soon-to-be major league pitcher and the dream of every young man's eye about to walk toward that elusive sunset arm in arm.

I was about to win the lottery before there had ever been one in our part of the world.

Then it happened.

I noticed it first in her sparkling auburn eyes as they slightly turned away to her left. I then turned in what seemed like slow motion to see my buddy Pug briskly scampering from the opposite side of the house. He was so excited as his slobbery tongue bounced in the wind and unlike me; he simply could not contain his emotions. I could sense what was about to happen, but somehow, I was defenseless ...I froze up. A moment that could possibly change history was about to happen and I simply could not prevent Pug from becoming the canine version of the Welcome Wagon for our neighborhood.

The angelic expression on her face now slowly was turning to a harsh shade of *Texas Chainsaw Massacre* horror as Pug made those final ten feet or so of his journey in midair. He now had his arms firmly wrapped around her neck and had placed a couple of extremely lathered tongue kisses to her face as I reach to pull him off.

It was at this exact moment that the unthinkable occurred.

Pug, my trusty friend and companion, had suddenly decided to take their newfound relationship to the, oh shall we say, next level. The angel of my eyes was now starting to spin counterclockwise rather briskly in an attempt to break free from his increasingly firm bear-hug grip. I, in turn, am trying to grab hold of Pug, while Pug is proceeding to do what comes very naturally to a dog of the male persuasion when so moved. He has her, I now have him, and we're spinning like a never-before-seen figure-skating threesome at the Olympics. Finally, with all the strength I can muster, I was able to pry his hunching mutt-self away and tackle him to the ground.

I am now holding Pug as I look up to see her wiping doggie slobber off her cheeks and adjusting her clothes and hair, trying to gather what is left of her dignity. As for me, I had just witnessed the end of what could have possibly been a beautiful, lifelong, Nicholas Sparks-inspired relationship in the matter of ten death-spinning seconds or so.

Pug had defiled my dream, and I knew now it was simply not meant to be.

Fighting back tears, she said her good-bye and limped slowly back down the hill. I'm sure she didn't fight back those tears as she made the journey. I can almost picture her making her way past the security guards equipped with assault rifles, wiping her face as she entered her tightly secured home.

Pug and I didn't speak to each other for days.

A year later, she and her family would move ...I was still too scarred to say good-bye. I think of that moment every so often. Did Pug interfere with the big plan, or was it just destiny?

I like to think it was just destiny.

She and I met back up on Facebook a few years ago, and she's still a very beautiful and now happily married lady. I didn't bring up the "incident," and thankfully, neither did she. I'm hopeful that it was a moment in time that she has been able to black out from her memory bank. As for me, it ranks right up there as one of the most startling and life-altering events of my life.

The next day, I gave up four runs in the backyard. Trust me, I was shocked too. It would take a while for me to get my confidence back.

They tell me it happens to all the great ones.

This Lake They Call Lula

She was seventeen with a head full of curls and a laugh that could fill the hollow that she grew up in. I can just hear that laugh now as she makes the hike through the briar-laden trails and steep hills adorned with rough, sometimes moss-covered rocks toward this place on the mountain, this special place ...at this lake they call Lula.

By my estimation it is 1930, and the Great Depression is just underway. But when you've always been poor, how are you supposed to know?

She makes her way with her girlfriends to a gathering of large boulders surrounding this small crystal-blue pool fed by a never-ending waterfall. It was probably the most beautiful sight she had ever seen, this lake they called Lula.

It's now sixty-seven years later. She is resting in her hospital bed as she nears her final days, her mind now covered with the thick veil of age. The stories of her life will soon be leaving with her. It's such a shame that we can sometimes leave this world with untold stories.

But not this day.

The fog suddenly lifts. She's not through yet; the lady has a story to tell. Now, the words of long ago begin to flow like water from an old spigot to anyone lucky enough to be within earshot of that hospital room.

She begins to recall that it was a beautiful day, but more than just that—it was a day that the sun changed the complexion of all it met with its celestial brush. The skies, oh the skies, they were simply a blue that she had never seen, perhaps because this color did not exist before that day. This place was magic, especially to a poor little girl from down in the valley.

From her bed, she waves her hands like a child again and begins to giggle as she describes the next event. The excitement is building, filling the room.

She's now sitting on those rocks with her girlfriends. In my mind, I see them all adorned in white cotton that almost glows from the warm sun as they kick their feet in the frigid water and toss rocks toward the falls.

One of the girls looks toward the brightness with a startled yet very pleased gaze. This movement catches the attention of the young girl with curls in her hair, and as she turns to look, a striking young man steps between her and the resplendent brilliance of the sun. A soft amber glow totally encompasses him ...a moment she would now recall all these years later with absolute certainty and clearness.

She doesn't realize it yet, but she has seen her future in this handsome twenty-four-year-old man. An older man who you just know heard the laugh and saw the smile of this beautiful girl at this lake they call Lula.

Within two years they would be married.

She would giggle a little longer as a grandson lapped up the words ...words about a grandfather that he never knew. He would die after a long, grueling illness in 1946 at the age of thirty-nine, leaving a wife of thirty-three and four little kids wanting to hear more stories. He left ten years before this grandson; his very first grandchild would be born.

Soon the fog returned, and this time it would settle in for good. The lady had spoken.

I found myself recalling that story last week when I heard that Lula Lake would be open on Saturday. The lake is part of a privately owned four-thousand-acre preserve on Lookout Mountain in northwest Georgia ...hidden from the world down an old railroad bed and protected thankfully now by the Lula Lake Land Trust. They open it on the first and last Saturdays of the month for hikers to enjoy.

I haven't done much hiking in my life, but I had an over-whelming feeling that I had to go ...I had to see this place for the very first time.

A few days later, I ventured up the mountain with a couple of good buddies. They both had experienced this adventure on several occasions, and they knew exactly why I wanted to come.

The skies were the color of burnt charcoal and gave no semblance of parting as we pulled up near the entrance. We made our way over to the trail marker, and soon we were hiking the same paths that I am most certain my grandfather, Paul Forrester, walked that very day ...that day now eighty-some odd years ago. I found myself looking more at the trail than the scenery much of the time. It was as if I was actually getting to walk where he had walked and be where he had been.

Finally, after a mile or so up steep hills and down winding paths, we began to hear water. All of a sudden I felt like a kid playing in the woods again, and the excitement was building as we picked up the pace just a bit. At last, the falls and the lake were in view, nestled between huge chasms of rocks. I now can bear witness that it's the most beautiful little lake your eyes will ever see on this side of the clouds ...this lake they call Lula.

I stood there for the longest looking down at this place that I always knew existed, but I had never actually visited. This place that is such a part of who I am. My gosh, a place that if it didn't exist ...I probably wouldn't, either.

Finally, I worked my way down the trail, carefully maneuvering among slick rocks until I made it to the spot, the spot you see in the picture ...the spot that I'm most certain Willie Mae Simpson was sitting and laughing as the sun grabbed her and Paul and simply never let go.

I'm not letting go either.

Play Me One

I was walking down Fourth Avenue down to Broadway in downtown Nashville the other day. It's a familiar area for me, and I love to drop by most any chance I get.

Now, I will most heartily admit, it's not what it used to be. I can remember some twenty-five years ago or so that you didn't readily visit this area without a friend, a weapon, or hopefully both. It had that feel, possibly what Bedford Falls would have been like if George Bailey hadn't saved his brother, Harry. Yep, Pottersville ...complete with a wayward Violet Biggs or two up near Tootsie's to complete the picture.

Progress and new money has transformed this historic area into Nashville's very own "Honky Tonk Bourbon Street." I still love it there, but it has become even more, let's just say, "touristy" than in days past. If someone had told me back in the mid-eighties as I was stepping over a couple of gentlemen obviously still sleeping one off from the night before, while gently ignoring a questionable lady just ahead and on my left, that one day there would be a Margaritaville restaurant and kids running freely up and down this very sidewalk...well, you know what I would have uttered.

Call me crazy, but in some ways I miss the old Broadway. Sometimes soap and water and paint can remove the character ...the patina if you will. But, you can't fight progress, so they say.

Back to my walk.

As I turned the corner from Fourth, there he was ...leaned back against a wall, his guitar resting comfortably against his chest, as he practiced his craft, just outside Gruhn's music store.

I was thankfully in not much of a hurry that day, and so I stopped as he concluded his latest ballad and struck up a conversation with him. We talked for a little while about life and about music, and he eventually opened up and told me that he was originally from Malvern, Arkansas. By the way, Malvern is the home of Billy Bob Thornton.

As we talked, he told me he writes and he sings for that most classic of reasons ...

"It's just something I gotta do."

I noticed he was playing an old Alvarez that, like him, had seen better days, but it fit him well. It was worn and faded to a rusty shade of yellow and truthfully, that top string could use just a little more adjusting, but it was close enough. I tossed a soft and somewhat stretched compliment about the guitar into the conversation, and he was quick to tell me, "Yeah, but it's got a Martin bridge."

He told me that a buddy of his was a luthier there at Gruhn's and had installed it for him.

He is so proud of that bridge.

It's kind of ironic—that bridge was kind of a connection from who is to what he wants to be. In a strange way, it made him a "somebody" in the music business ...not just another slightly inebriated guy strumming on a cheap guitar for tips.

"Play me one," I urged him as I dropped some money in his case.

He strummed around slowly for a while as his mind was racing, and then he proceeded to lean back just a bit, close his eyes, and belt out a tearjerker ..."I'm Real Easy to Lose."

By the way, it was a good one ...I'm talking a really good one.

He finished the last verse, ran that C lick into the chorus one more time, and then took it home with a turnaround. I gave him a one-person ovation, as those passing by were simply too busy looking for another shop to purchase some official trinkets. If they had just stopped for a second, they would have realized that the very heart of this town had just been on display for the last three minutes.

It's the music.

I wanted to know more about the song—surely there was a story behind the story. He told me that he wrote it one cold and rainy night sheltered under the awning of a building just across the street ...up near Ernest Tubb's record shop. Surprisingly, it wasn't really about any one girl in particular. He kinda laughed when he said that a broken heart makes it easier to write a song.

He pointed to his chest and told me, "This one's been broken several times."

I love songs that you can absolutely feel the truth and emotion pouring out through the strings. Songs that reach out and grab you ...'cause that's what things from the heart do.

They write 'em every day up there, but very few get out. Business and creativity have just never been very good partners.

That's such a shame.

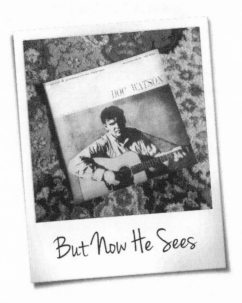

But Now He Sees

Doc Watson passed away tonight.

To many, that name will be unfamiliar, while others will define him as a guitar player. This is true, but Doc was not just a guitar player. To be more specific, he was a flatpicker ...but then to simply say that is like saying Rembrandt or Cézanne were painters. You just feel there needs to be some more descriptive words added.

Doc won numerous Grammys, and his musical influence reached all around the world. He passed away almost two months to the day after Earl Scruggs's death, and they were truly two of the most influential and respected acoustic musicians to ever walk on this planet. Doc and Earl were almost the same age, lifelong friends, and folks will discuss and analyze their music long after I'm gone. They didn't just carve a unique musical path throughout the years, they went four lanes ...and they did it with style and grace.

Earl, Levon Helm, and now Doc in a two-month period. It seems they're all leaving us.

The night Earl passed away, I wrote about the time, around 1981, when I got to see and meet him. It was at a music hall that used to be down near the river, just off Market Street in Chattanooga. Ironically, it was just a few months before that meeting that I got to see Doc Watson at that very same music hall. My buddies and I had basically the exact same great seats to see Doc in action.

Now, keep in mind, these were the days before the Internet and the wealth of information readily available to us at our fingertips. All we knew about Doc was his music, which we had *heard*. My first introduction to Doc was through the very first bluegrass album I ever owned, *Will the Circle Be Unbroken* by the Nitty Gritty Dirt Band. I was amazed at the intricate sounds emitting from the album as it scratched through my old Motorola stereo. I cannot even begin to count the number of times I would sit and listen to that entire album. Later on, I can remember sitting around with my buddy David Jones and we would sing "Tennessee Stud" as he would attempt to hit the notes that Doc was able to swiftly muster from a six string.

Move forward to that spring night in 1981 as we stood up from our seats in the wings just off stage left to applaud Doc and his son Merle as they entered and made their way to the stage. Doc entered like a prizefighter following Merle (also a superb guitar player who would die in a tractor accident just a few years later). Doc's right hand grasped Merle's right shoulder as they made their way through the crowd from our left. I can still remember the moment I noticed it and turned to one of my buddies, who had noticed it at the same time ..."My gosh, Doc Watson is blind!" Until that night and until that moment, we had absolutely no idea.

Doc and Merle—whom Doc named after his friend and legendary musician Merle Travis—finally made it to the stage, along with a bass player. They got themselves all situated and then proceeded to put on a show that originated the term "shock and awe." I sat there the whole night amazed at what I was seeing and equally amazed that he was performing music at this level without the benefit of sight.

There are two things I think of often from that night, other than the music. One, I would learn that not only was Doc blind, but he wired his own house. I have two good eyes, and I feel proud of myself when I stick an extension cord into a socket. The other was a feat that amazes me to this day, and anyone who was there that night I'm sure remembers it vividly. Merle was taking a break during one of the songs, and as he was picking, he accidentally knocked his longneck beer over. Without missing a lick, he tapped the end of the beer bottle with his foot, and it stood right back up in its proper position. The crowd went crazy. I honestly don't think he spilled a drop or missed a note.

Doc was a multitalented individual and by all accounts a kind, generous, and wonderful man. But tonight, I'm not thinking about the music. Truthfully, I can only think of one thing ...can you just imagine what Doc can see now?

I bet he doesn't blink for a thousand years.

Just Let It Slam

The back door at Mama's was protected by a slamming screen door that not only kept out the flies, but allowed the aromas from her kitchen to reach out to the neighborhood and on toward the heavens around suppertime every night. Truthfully, I pretty much just described every single house even remotely near me in the early seventies. Looking back, it seemed as though there was a steady rhythm, the sun acting much like a metronome for life in our part of the world. But, you started hearing about a new product for the home back then, one that most people, including Mama, eventually bought into ...storm doors. Of course, they were nothing more than fancy screen doors with glass coverings, but they had a carefully engineered closer that enabled the door to make a somewhat smooth transition back to its resting place, thus saving the glass. As the years went on, you didn't hear screen doors slam much anymore. When the screen doors left, so did most of the lightning bugs. Our timing was now off. The rhythm was somehow gone. Suddenly, being outside just wasn't as important anymore.

Years later, after I had married and put away childish memories, Mama got a new door to replace that modern storm door leading out to the carport. It was a very nice screen door with Victorian-style elements. It was kind of heavy too, offering a good slam. I was there when Daddy installed it, and I had forgotten just how perfect that sound was.

It's years later now and we just built a new screened-in back porch at our house. As usual, I had no say-so about such things, but this time I did make one small request. There would be screen doors on each end. Screen doors that I wanted wound tightly enough to be heard slamming down to the Shop-Rite and over to the Smokehouse, just behind us on Thomas Avenue. My demanding wish was granted. Then, I started praying for the lightning bugs to bring a whole bunch of their buddies with them when they come back next year.

I keep slamming those doors. I just know they're out there listening.

Mama died in the summertime. Later that year, it would have been around this time as the leaves were beginning to change colors and eventually lose grip on their home, Daddy began working on his kitchen ...actually Mama's kitchen, it always was. There was no announcement, and he began the transformation rather quietly without any paint, new appliances, new flooring or any of those other things you might find on one of those HGTV remodeling programs. He simply started incorporating apples into the decor. Apple plates, apple pictures, apple towels, apple magnets on the refrigerator ...pretty much anything he could find apple-related he bought and found a spot for it. He then took a trip over to Ellijay, the apple capital of Georgia and loaded his truck up with so many apple-themed decor items, that he finally could no longer find any open places to put them. I remember finding it humorous, and a little odd that my dad had suddenly developed such a keen eye for interior design. He was very proud of his work, his newly found skills if you will. I, on the other hand, began to entertain thoughts that perhaps Daddy's losing it.

Then, one afternoon I dropped by to see him on my way home from work. As I walked through the carport, I was suddenly engulfed with the most wonderful smell of apples as they wafted through the screen and out into the neighborhood. I can take you today to that very spot where the fragrance met me. Apple-scented candles, those glorious bottles of wax that can take your mind back to special times. The sense of smell somehow just doesn't forget, and for me, it is a very intense remembrance, almost like a time-travel moment ...if only for a few seconds at a time. Mama loved the smell of apple-spice in the kitchen as the cool mornings arrived. I can still remember those apple candles lighting up the darkness after all the plates had been washed and put away at night. Then, the warming aroma of leaves burning throughout the neighborhood, their crackles and woody smoke adding yet another layer to the autumnal palette.

Daddy remembered too.

That spicy apple scent accompanied me as I walked through the carport and finally pulled the screen door open. As I entered the kitchen, I felt as if I was walking back to another time ...then the door slammed behind me. It was at that very moment that I finally realized what had happened. Daddy hadn't just fancied up the kitchen, he was trying with everything he had to bring back and hold on intensely to memories of Mama. We never spoke about it, we didn't have to.

Mama was still there and to this day, she's never left me.

So, today, I ventured over to the big town, strolled into the big mall and walked right into the candle store and laid some cold, hard cash down for a *Mama-in-a-Jar*. I do it around this time every year.

I came back home, lit the wick, closed my eyes and took a deep smell all the way back to that kitchen. Then, I went out onto the back porch, opened the screen door and just let it slam. Daddy would have liked that.

Yep, it's gonna be another wonderful Fall y'all.

The Greatest Fight
I Never Saw

I am going to tell you a story that is not only true, but the words I will write will be totally void of exaggeration, scattered only with possible name changes to protect, as they say, the "innocent." I was there and I witnessed it. Yes, each and every event of that evening was recorded for further review by my own deep and somewhat piercing green eyes.

Wait, wait, let me correct myself. Truthfully, I witnessed each and every event of this particular night except for one maybe five-second sequence when my view was blocked by a couple of other witnesses to history.

Now, having said all of that, I feel that I must also inform you that I still have the evidence, henceforth known as exhibit A, which indeed is further proof that this event most certainly did occur.

I will be taking you back to events that transpired in a bar—a watering hole if you will—in a town not unlike, oh, shall we say, Chattanooga, Tennessee. The hostages had just been taken in Iran, Jimmy Carter was president, "We Are Family" was all over the airwaves, and the Pirates had just captured the World Series. It's the fall of 1979.

Sit back and relax as we return to the scene of the greatest fight I never saw.

Let me start out by saying I have never been one for fighting. Yes, I have come close several times in my life, but never have I thrown a punch in anger, nor has a punch reached this lovely face of my mama's only child.

I did find myself once in the middle of one of the greatest fights in local baseball history at the old Darwin Field in East Lake. It was on a Sunday afternoon that was so bright I have to squint even now when I think back on it. Both teams, several coaches, and finally one crazed parent all going at it on an infield the color of sugar, in ninety-plus degree heat, right smack dab in the middle of July. Truthfully, I spent those anxious moments dodging punches and basically practicing the fine art of self-defense as mayhem reminiscent of a saloon fight in western days ensued all around me. I swear I heard whiskey bottles breaking and bar stools a-flying, all while the piano player kept playing …well, at least it seemed that way. By the time the police had arrived and helped separate the teams and the final siren was flipped off, the only person with any measurable damage was that aforementioned crazed parent who ran into the middle of the melee. I was no more than five feet away when a single punch spread his nose from ear to ear. One punch from one of my teammates, who happens to be a very good buddy of mine to this very day.

Back to 1979.

It's a cool fall Saturday night, as I recall it had rained that afternoon. We all met at Peanut's, our usual gathering spot over in Spencer Hills to head as a group into Chattanooga for a night of bluegrass music, beer, and the occasional lady or two at Dac's, our favorite place to just be. We had a Jeep full ...Robbie (our official leader at all times), David, who everyone called Rat, Frank, and me. Each of us was wearing cowboy hats (curse you, John Travolta, and your Urban Cowboy trend) and was ready to raise some quasi-Hades. Everything is a go, and we're about to head out when another buddy shows up ...Big Dave.

Big Dave, the same guy who once got mad late one night, hopped out of our vehicle, and proceeded to beat up a totally defenseless stop sign. In a fit of rage, he beat it all the way to the ground, and if I'm not mistaken, we finally pulled him off of it. That poor sign did nothing to deserve it and truthfully never saw it coming.

Big Dave, the former bouncer at one of the biggest night-spots in town and who on a consistent weekend basis, served up almost as many posterior whoopins as beers sold and phone numbers exchanged at the club.

Big Dave, who once got kicked out of an intramural football game in college, for, let us just say, unnecessary roughness. Then, after further review, the school would determine that this star defensive lineman on our team was technically not an actual student of said institution in the truest sense of the word.

That Big Dave.

It seemed that wherever Big Dave went, trouble was usually already there and had possibly had a few, or trouble was well on its way and should be there any minute. Let's just say trouble and Big Dave had several confrontations back in those days.

I can still remember the "Look, we're going to have some fun, drink some beer, and listen to music. We don't want any trouble" speech that was given, as we got ready to head over into the big town. Big Dave agreed and said he'd meet us there.

When we arrived and burst through the front door of Dac's, we were pleased to see that not only was our booth available, but also it seemed to be very happy to see us. Our booth, the one at the very front—right near the stage and all the action. Now, those booths were really big and handmade out of treated two-by-sixes. They sat eight and were built as one piece. Solid as a granite monument. As an added bonus, you could sit on the very top of the back of the seats for an even better view of the band, as I oft did.

The beer was cold, cheap, and served in pitchers. I've always found that quite proper. The music was perfect for singing along, especially if you knew the words. Another interesting feature was the fact that the men's bathroom door never shut, because the urinal was equipped with a specially made roulette wheel. Of course, this provided a very enticing target for the customer at that particular moment and endless entertainment for others waiting their turn. Yep, people really would watch and make imaginary bets as the participant was relieving himself. Both men and women enjoyed the game. We're talking high-class entertainment.

Dang, I loved that place.

We're kicked back in our booth, and I'm sure I had already assumed my perch up on the back of the seat. The pitchers were flowing, the music was at the proper tempo...the lyrics of which I most certainly was familiar with, and I most likely was proudly demonstrating my vocal talents for anyone nearby. David, Frank, and I had our own unique three-part harmony. It was basically a unique mix of a fairly consistent two-part, along with an accidental third hit about every third or fourth note or so. We were having our usual perfect night, in our very own perfect part of the world.

Then they walked in.

I noticed them immediately. They seemed to walk in at a thirty-three speed when the rest of us were carrying on at forty-five, well on our way to seventy-eight (you youngsters may not get the reference; just give it a Google). Three guys—three rough guys—and it was most apparent they were members of some sort of a motorcycle gang. Now, keep in mind, this was before bike rallies and Christmas toy runs and before Harley-Davidson became somewhat of a status symbol. Back then, if you were in a motorcycle gang, in my mind you ranked right up there with Charles Manson. You were badness personified.

"Look, take anything you want, just don't hurt me." That was my general attitude toward them and truthfully, a mantra I carry to this very day.

The booth to my immediate left over against the wall was available, and they slowly approached it, taking possession like pirates returning from sea to celebrate their ill-gotten gains. This was their property now, they owned the space, and you can't even view it again ...at least don't let them catch you viewing it.

We all noticed them, but nothing was said ...who knew, they may have acquired special lip-reading abilities while they were out there pillaging. We for sure knew that they had not made off with any grooming gels and colognes. All we needed to do now was just mind our own business and enjoy the other 98 percent of space left there at Dac's.

So, there we were, having our typical livin' large, good ol' boy, Saturday night in the South ...but that was soon to change.

Now, we come to that place I've been working to get you to from the very beginning.

It seems that our buddies had decided to take a slow walk to the back to try their luck and skill at the pinball machines. As they left our sight, it soon became very apparent that one of the trio had obviously either a) had consumed too much alcohol or perhaps b) had not had a good night's sleep the night before. This remaining biker dude was lying with his face flat down on the table in absolute dreamland, just like a freshly powdered newborn.

We suddenly found ourselves squarely in that most awkward of positions ...you know the one, it's like when something really funny happens at a funeral. Laughing out loud is just not an option; it would be the ultimate faux pas. In our case, it could also mean possibly severe bodily injury.

We looked over there several times and snickered under our breath. It was hilarious, I'm telling you, you just had to be there. Good, clean, wholesome fun.

Then here it came ...trouble. I told you it would be here shortly.

As much fun as we were having, for some reason Big Dave couldn't just let it go, no ...he had to take it to the next level. The next thing we know, he takes a few steps over to their booth, sits down opposite of said passed-out biker dude, pours himself a beer, and proceeds to act like he's having a conversation with him. We're laughing hysterically—the key is—on the inside. On the outside, I'm sure we each possessed that look of possible doom that surely awaited us. Finally, Big Dave comes back to our booth, and it's over ...whew. Let's just forget about those guys and get back to enjoying everything else.

Before we could commence to doing just that, they came back. Not only did they come back but also it became very evident, very quickly, that they had witnessed the events that had just transpired—the obvious mocking of their obviously over-served compadre. Someone would have to pay. Please just don't let it be me.

Their leader, a somewhat stocky and violently rough-looking individual, with a head full of hair that resembled orange steel wool along with an equally distasteful matching beard, hollered over toward our table and basically made several derogatory comments at Big Dave. In fact, he inferred several things about Big Dave's ancestry that I, for one, found quite appalling. Let's face it—they had never even been officially

---

introduced, so how could he have been privy to such personal information? Mr. Motorcycle Gang Leader was making far too many assumptions, in my opinion.

Now, the more sailor-influenced comments he tossed our way, the more you could see Big Dave starting to resemble one of those Looney Tunes cartoon characters on the verge of exploding. He sat there with his hands clinched, and they were beginning to violently shake as they started bouncing off the table. It was about this time that I'm starting to feel the possibility that this could be the very night that my face finally feels violence viciously thrust upon it.

Tension, anger, testosterone, and good ol' machismo were swirling around like spices in a Thanksgiving morning kitchen when finally these words were uttered by Mr. Motorcycle Gang Leader:

"Let's take this outside, big boy!"

Big Dave turned toward him and gleefully spoke the single baddest word I've ever heard in the history of my life:

"Let's."

They both jumped up from their booths, like boxers from corner stools, and headed toward the door. Crowds of spectators were making their way toward the door as well. I stood up in my seat to catch the view before I got down to go outside. I remember then seeing a slight scuffle. An arm came above the crowd and back down into it. It was at that precise moment that the air was pierced with an unbelievably moaning scream.

Truthfully, it was an odd noise. As I recall, it wasn't like a girly scream or one, say, from a little kid ...it was more like that of a grown man reduced to his early teen years in the matter of oh, shall we say, two to three seconds. The ruckus was over that quickly, and everyone started returning to their booths. As for me, I found myself in that somewhat at times familiar state of bewilderment as Big Dave stomped back toward our camp.

What just happened?

It was then that he threw something at me, which I caught with both hands. I can remember distinctly looking into them with a bit of confusion. What was this, and where had it come from?

I looked toward Mr. Motorcycle Gang Leader as he made his way back to his booth, his hands clutching the left side of his face, which now possessed a look of inconsolability. I looked back at my hands, to Big Dave, to the rest of the table, back over to the motorcycle dudes, and then, with horror and without uttering a word, I knew exactly what had just happened.

I now was in possession of the left side—meaning one half—of what used to be the complete beard of Mr. Motorcycle Gang Leader. I didn't know if I was supposed to give it back to him, pass it around the room, or hoist it as a trophy like the gladiators of old. Honestly, I like to think that most of us are ill equipped as to what to do in that particular situation. So, I just sat there in awe. You just know something incredible has just happened, but who is going to believe it? I guess it's kind of like how those guys in the trailer park who just saw a UFO feel.

Slowly the motorcycle dudes got up to leave, gathering their coats and what was left of their dignity as Mr. Motorcycle Gang Leader held his face and headed dejectedly toward the door.

DALE FORRESTER

As they made their way to the sidewalk, Mr. Motorcycle Gang Leader spoke his famous last words to Robbie:

"Hey man, your buddy ain't cool."

With that, they hopped on their big bikes and sped away into the remainder of the night. One can only imagine the pain that awaited Mr. Motorcycle Gang Leader the next morning when he woke up to a sober world.

So, there you have it ...a stone-cold, true story from top to bottom. Now, looking back, I didn't even change the names. Oh yeah, and one more thing ...I guess now you understand Exhibit A.

Dang, I loved that place.

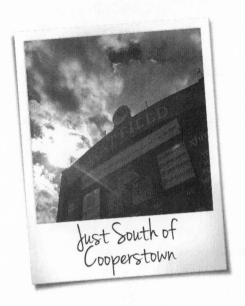

Just South of Cooperstown

Yesterday, I got to take a special trip to a wonderful place that I have wanted to visit for quite some time now. You know that place I'm talking about. Sure, there are different names for it ... as for me; I like to refer to it as "Back in the Day."

It was as if me and one of my all-time best buddies, Robbie Robertson, had hopped into a DeLorean and entered "October 10, 1977" into the controls, filled the flux capacitor up with plutonium (yeah, we stole it from some Libyans), kicked it up to eighty-eight mph, and went *Back to the Future*.

We were given the opportunity to play ball at the home of the Chattanooga Lookouts, our AA minor league team—beautiful AT&T Field, with its crayon-green grass perfectly combed and manicured and the infield dirt groomed like a Sunday bunker at Augusta. It was a fall afternoon, and God purposely chose to push aside the cotton-ball clouds that had covered us since the weekend for just this moment, just for a little while. A loving act that would allow some special folks up there the opportunity to have the absolute best seats in the house. Yep, that's what I believe and I double-dog dare you to try and prove me wrong.

We ran—actually, it was a slightly aggressive walk—to the outfield and warmed up by simply soft-tossing a baseball back and forth. Sure, we stretched some, but not too much ...we didn't want to actually pull a muscle while stretching to try and prevent pulling a muscle. Trust me, the irony of such an event would have been spoken of in sarcastic tones around these parts for the rest of my days.

We soon were shagging fly balls, fielding grounders, and laughing often at our total lack of range. You know, the weird thing about playing baseball to me is that when you are on a ball field, for the rest of your life, you know exactly in your mind what you're supposed to do and how to do it. Why? Because in my opinion, baseball is a collection of skills ...learned skills, mixed with some athletic ability. Now, I was fortunate to have some wonderful coaches over the years who taught me things ...some I could do well, and some—well, let's just say there's a reason not everybody gets to play on TV.

Now, knowing what to do and actually performing the task are two totally different subjects. I have found that as you get older, your mind and this much-more-mature body that you now possess do not communicate nearly as well as I feel they should. Actually, the mind still does its part ...the body, well, therein lies the problem.

Finally, it was my turn. My very first turn in the batting cage, a moment that for some reason I had no idea how much I wanted until I found out I would have the opportunity. Wooden bats, the way God and Mr. Doubleday intended—wooden bats that I had not swung in over thirty-five years—and live pitching ...for goodness' sake, anybody can hit a blame pitching machine consistently.

I slowly made my way into the cage and dug in, holding an Old Hickory size 33.5, a good size. A few deep breaths, and the first pitch was on its way. Now, I would like to say I lined it back up the middle, or perhaps dusted the left field line for extra bases. Truthfully, I topped it into the dirt ...but, I made contact, and I didn't hurt myself in the process.

So far, so good.

Soon, I was indeed, on occasion, lining balls to different parts of the field, and yes, I even got into a few. Connecting with the sweet spot on a good wooden bat is still a true moment of ecstasy, similar to warm Krispy Kremes or sliding under flannel sheets on a cold January night. It just flat-out feels good ... forget the descriptives.

I got several turns throughout the day, and I'm here to tell you, being between the foul lines is still one of the greatest places to be on this earth. Robbie would take several turns in the cage as well, and yes, he hit it just a bit farther at times ... he always could.

Overall, we put the ball in play consistently, we fielded our positions as well as could be expected, and we didn't finish the day on the DL. Hey, I've been watching the playoffs this week, and the way I look at it, we had a better day than A-Rod has been having all week long, and for anyone interested, Robbie and I would do it again at a fraction of his cost.

Yes, it was a glorious day, and yes, I was eighteen again ... if only for just a little while. If you want to know the truth, I wouldn't want to go back to that age for a long period of time anyway.

I'm hoping Russell and Sonny were proud ...but you know, I have a pretty good feeling they had just as much fun as we did. Again, my double-dog dare challenge is still out there.

On a side note, I caught myself still dropping that back shoulder at times ...gotta work on that.

He Got Away

Every generation has one, you know, the one that got away.

"You better slow down!"

I remember where I was standing ...I venture to say I could take you very near to the exact spot when I hollered those words. I can show you where he was sitting, straddling that motorcycle across the street in his driveway.

It's the fall of 1978; December to be exact ...Christmas was approaching. It was the second Thursday of the month.

I first met him when we moved to Mountain View in the spring of 1969. We moved into a brick rancher there on Lewis Street, a house that sat across the street from his.

I think of those days often ...I have spoken many times of how much I loved that place. It was a big subdivision with our own swimming pool and our own school, and every house had at least a kid or two. You had to go up a hill to get anywhere.

When I finally left there years later, I swore I would never live on a hill again.

That place simply never leaves me.

"Tell him to come eat supper with us."

Mom was always concerned about him. I didn't understand it then, but these many years later, it is perfectly clear to me.

Even though he lived across the street, he would spend the night with me often during those days. We would camp out during the summer, and about every night we played ball down at Bradford's field until we wore grassy areas down to the dirt. Baseball, football, basketball ...whatever was in season. Mr. Bradford would come out and play with us sometimes. He was a good man.

We played rec baseball and church basketball together, and we were members of the very first Mountain View Gators football team. For three years he was the center and I was the quarterback. He would always wear a towel tucked in the back of his pants so I could wipe my hands on it before I called signals. We saw that on TV and thought it looked cool. He wore #55 and I wore #10. We loved the Vols ...Bobby Scott, Steve Kiner, Bobby Majors, and Curt Watson. Heck, we even had General Neyland's grandson on our team. He lived just around the corner.

• • •

"Son, wake up...He's been in a wreck."

It was early on a sunny Saturday morning—early in those days meant 8:15 for me. He had been in a wreck a few hours before, crashing a brand-new yellow Corvette. Truthfully, he was doing something he shouldn't, at a place he shouldn't have been, at a time when nothing good happens. It was December 2, 1978.

"He's gonna be OK."

I remember trying to wake up and process what I had just heard. The words I spoke next my dad would repeat often throughout the years.

"That's the way he'll go."

Yes, I remember every single second of that brief conversation. It seemed now that the clock was officially ticking down, and I could plainly hear it.

Truthfully, he had dodged one ...I just hoped he could dodge another.

• • •

"Just be careful."

It was a Thursday afternoon. I remember the orange glow of the sun as it was slowly sliding behind Crest Ridge Drive up the hill from us. He laughed as he hollered back to me from just down the hill and across the street.

"I'll be careful!"

He sat there straddling his motorcycle and adjusting his helmet. Yes, motorcycles can be dangerous, more so when guided by a nineteen year old with newfound money and an air of invincibility. A new Datsun 240Z straight off the showroom floor was now sitting beside him in the driveway. Just another toy.

As I look back now, it's as if for a few weeks that same clock that I could hear ticking down was now moving at twice its normal speed. You could only sit there, helpless to slow it down, as you watched the events unfold at the house across the street.

It's Friday night, December 15, and it's raining ...a downpour that at times the wipers on my '74 Ford Pinto Wagon simply could not keep up with. For some reason, I came back home early that night, down my usual course along Mission Ridge Road. I'm sure I was home by 11:30, safe and dry. Christmas shopping was most likely on the agenda for the next day.

"Good night, Mama."

Lightning and thunder accompanied me as I lay my head down. Rain has always helped me sleep well.

There was a knock, and the door opened in my bedroom. It must have been around 7:00 that next morning. It's Saturday, and I can remember rising up to see my dad, eerily in the exact same position he had been in on that Saturday two weeks before. Now, looking back, it seems I was already prepared for the words.

"He's been in a wreck again."

"Is he OK?" I asked, although I knew the answer before I asked the question.

My dad simply shook his head slowly.

I got up, hurriedly dressed, and headed to the scene of the wreck. A crowd was already there at the crash site.

We did things like that back then.

It seems he had traveled that same Mission Ridge Road sometime in the early morning, hours after I had since passed by ...only he was heading in the opposite direction at a speed hitting near triple digits, according to the report. He lost control in a curve, swerved off the road and then back, and finally, he catapulted off the asphalt, taking a dormer off the second story of a house before landing.

That new 240Z was new no more.

There was now a calmness that it seemed had been missing for some time. The rain had stopped, but the clouds remained and that same clock that had been spinning almost out of control slowed back down as if it was righting itself to its proper speed.

Folks would talk about that dormer for years.

I was there the following night at the hospital when his mother made the gut-wrenching decision to "pull the plug." I had already visited with him once, and now I was asked if I would like to go back one more time ...this time to say goodbye. The visuals of that moment are still with me as well as the sounds of those machines. I simply wasn't ready for a moment like this, but then, who is?

Yes indeed, every generation has one.

Thirty-four years ago today one of my best childhood buddies simply got away before we could grab him, and I wanted you to know that.

The Brown Paper Bag

Maybe I was four years old, yep, we'll go with that.

With that thought in mind, it is the Christmas season of 1963, and I'm at my grandparents' house on Salem Road in Rossville. It was a very small, white frame house ...most likely built sometime in the 1920s. I'm thinking it was maybe seven hundred square feet if you stretched the tape measure just a bit and fudged some. Looking back, I'm amazed how many family members we could squeeze into that little place on Christmas Eve each year.

It just never seemed small.

This particular Christmas season, my grandmother took me to Salem Road Baptist Church for a special Christmas program. Honestly, I remember very little about it. Oh, I'm sure there was plenty of singing, there was probably some sort of nativity scene, and I'm quite sure there would have been an old white-haired man who probably got up and read from the book of Luke about there being "suddenly a great company of the heavenly host appearing with the angel." Yep, the birth of Jesus was probably discussed in great detail ...probably at times with the fullest of his energy.

Around here, we love emphasis.

No, I don't remember anything about the service, but truthfully, there is something that I do remember from that night. A night that existed before Neil Armstrong ever thought about walking on the moon, before the Braves would decide that Atlanta was a great place to raise a baseball team, and before I entered the first grade at Mountain View Elementary School.

At the end of the service, as we were filing out, there was a table at the entryway. I distinctly remember there were ladies standing there, each passing out brown paper bags to all the kids as we were leaving ...and they gave me one.

It would prove to be probably the greatest Christmas present I ever got.

Now, my granny's house was no more than a mile away from the church, and I don't remember the exact moment of opening the bag ...I only remember its contents. It contained an assortment of hard candies, some nuts still in the shell, and an orange. This was the earliest remembrance I have of getting a gift, and I can remember how special it made me feel. It was magical, I'm telling you ...even the bag looked special to me.

My granny had a wooden bowl on her coffee table, which had been carved out of a tree and lacquered up with the bark still on it. In the middle of the bowl was a stand that held some sort of metal contraption. I would find out that night that it was a nutcracker; she sat with me and showed me how to use it. I played with it for years, most every time I would find myself at the white frame house up on the hill, just off Salem Road.

Yes, it was a wonderful event in my life, but the thing that really stuck out the most, believe it or not, was that orange. Now, you have to remember that a little boy in the early sixties wasn't exposed to many oranges, at least not in my part of the world. I do not remember eating it, although surely I did. Actually the thing I remember most of all was the smell …that smell has stuck with me my entire life. I can remember holding it up to my nose and feeling the coarseness of the skin as I deeply inhaled it. It was hard, yet somewhat mushy at the same time.

To most, oranges are associated with Florida, California, or any other coastal destination, but for me, an orange reminds me of Christmas and a very special gift I received years and years ago.

That moment absolutely stays with me. It's part of the reason that to this day, at least once a year, I will venture out of my way just to drive down Salem Road one more time, an extremely curvy and somewhat hilly journey that will take me by where my granny's house once stood and then on past that old church. It's just something I have to do from time to time. I just do.

I brought you to this point to say this: we never know which memories will stick with us. They're made when somehow we least expect them, and I believe they shape us and help us to become who we are. These treasures, these nuggets in life that we carry with us, are simply not planned. They're your gift, and you need to remember that. I do every single time I see an orange.

Who knows what gifts we can offer that will impact a life ...gifts that show you care. It could be just a word you share, a simple deed you do ...or possibly just a little brown paper bag filled with less than a dollar's worth of trinkets.

Oh, don't you know the lady who handed me that bag that night would love to hear that?

Something tells me she just did.

Johnson Road Roy

I was a member of the Key Club at Rossville High School. Back then, you were either in the Key Club or the JE's. Looking back, it was kind of like our very own fraternity system complete with all the trappings and social events of one of those Greek life organizations minus the really cool house ...well, at least not an official one. I was probably a junior when our club advisor told us we had been given an opportunity to work at something I had never heard of at the time: the Special Olympics. It was all part of that whole working and giving back to the community commitment. Truthfully, you could get out of school for a whole day and take a slight road trip. Naturally, most of us Key Clubbers gleefully signed up. I mean, look, it was for the community.

Now, until that day, I had never really been around mentally handicapped people before, or, as we used to say, the "retards."

Sure, we had a couple at our school, and yes, I'm ashamed to say they were often easy targets of ridicule. We would make jokes from time to time about their mannerisms, the way they talked ...they were the defenseless ones that we could laugh at, and I guess in some ways this gave us a superior feeling.

I remember that day in some ways with startling detail. The Olympics were held at the old Wallaceville Junior High School just outside Chickamauga. As we got off the bus, there were these "special kids" running around everywhere, and there wasn't a single one not carrying a smile with them. Our advisor gathered us with some officials from the Games to give us our duties. I can specifically remember watching those "special kids" running and playing with the same enthusiasm we had back in elementary school, and I can remember being disappointed. This was not going to turn out well. We were just here to babysit.

I went to my area—honestly, I don't remember my duties. I'm standing there next to some of the "special" ones, and naturally a conversation got started. Soon, another one came, followed by another and within just a few seconds I had my own gang. I had some gum and they loved that, and we talked, and soon I was laughing and cutting up with them. We hugged a bunch and by a bunch, I mean a lot. I do not know why I can remember bits and pieces of that day ...that day that took place over thirty years ago. I learned an important fact and would remember it every time I got to go back ...candy and chewing gum was a big deal. Later times, I would bring pockets packed with sugary goodies.

Details of the day I do not remember ...but images I do. Smiles, constant smiles. Laughing even as they competed. Clapping all the time for whomever ...the first-place guy, the last-place girl ...it just didn't matter. They were totally happy; they were loving life, and oh how they loved everyone else. I had simply never seen anything like that in my whole life.

I can remember that night at the dinner table talking to my mom and dad. I believe if I think hard enough, I can even remember what we were eating. I told them about my day. I opened up, which was unusual for me at the time. I told them I was just not really sure who had this whole thing right. I promise I can almost hear that conversation today.

I truly left that day a different person. It affected me immensely and helped form the way I would coach ball teams for the next twenty-five years or so. I had learned to care more about kids getting to just play and be happy rather than the constant concern about runs or points on a scoreboard. If a kid wanted to try a position, I let him try. I never relegated a kid to the bench and tried to work him in when I could. I did my best to treat every kid the same, regardless of ability. They deserve that. I can trace it all back to a field full of kids living and loving life in a community called Wallaceville.

It was very possible that maybe these kids weren't the "crazy" ones—maybe it was us...the supposedly "normal" kids. Maybe these kids were "special" because they had been given that gift from God. They simply looked at things differently, maybe the way we were supposed to look at them. Whatever they had, they sure were a happy, carefree bunch.

I have never forgotten that day.

Years later, I moved just a few miles away to downtown Chickamauga. It was soon after that I met Roy, or as we refer to him, "Johnson Road Roy" ...he's the man in the picture. I had seen Roy for what seemed my whole life, but now we were official acquaintances, and I'm proud to say we would become friends. Now, you could talk to most anyone in our town and they would know who Roy was. They may not have met him, but they knew he was the guy who walked back and forth from Johnson Road into town every single day like clockwork. He could often be found sitting on the wall in front of the old Jewell mansion, or on the bench in front of the train depot. He arrived in the afternoon around suppertime, and he returned somehow just as the sun was setting. Among the other gifts God gave Roy, an inner clock was one of his most prized possessions.

I talk to Roy quite often. He passes my house most every single day. Our conversations are usually short, but we have had some in-depth ones. He worries often that I need to change my motor oil and check my transmission fluid.

One afternoon last year Roy stopped me as I was on one of my daily runs. Usually if he's on the wall as I run by, we will exchange a high-five ...I have my headphones on, and Roy knows I am focused. But on this day as we high-fived, Roy kind of held on. He wanted to talk. I stopped and pulled off my headphones.

Roy stood there, his smile gone ...an extremely rare occurrence for him. He had concern in his voice. Macho Man

Randy Savage—or as Roy always said, "Twelve-Time-World-Heavyweight-Champion Macho Man Randy Savage" —had died. We discussed what a great champion he was and how his bionic elbow could knock anybody out. Then Roy got more serious; he was worried sick for Elizabeth, Macho Man's wife, and he asked me to pray for her as I left him to continue my run. He was just so sincere in his request. I didn't have the heart or desire to tell him that not only had they divorced several years ago, but Elizabeth had passed away as well.

Now, I could fill a book full of Roy stories, and trust me, I have some good ones—especially from all those years at the ball fields—but here's what I want to leave you with.

The other night on one of my nightly runs, I passed Roy sitting there in his usual spot on the rock wall, and that's when it hit me. Just what goes through his mind on a typical day? We all have inner thoughts, and Roy has to be no different. When he smiles at a nice family, does he think inside "I wish that was my family"? When a nice new car passes by, does he ever wish he were driving? Does he want for or desire anything? Do these thoughts pass through his mind?

I have come to believe that they don't.

The apostle Paul considered this very subject when he wrote, "I have learned, in whatsoever state I am, therewith to be content." You see, Paul developed a quality that I have been absolutely unable to come close to grasping. No matter where he was and what was going on, Paul was content; he was happy. Why? Because Paul knew that this time we spend here on earth is just a blip on the screen; in fact, it doesn't even make a speck when compared to eternity. We believers have something waiting beyond.

Now, can Roy comprehend this? I believe in his own way, he most certainly can, and maybe that's why he smiles all the time. Maybe that's why a lot of those "special folks" we consider mentally handicapped are only handicapped by our standards ...perhaps they're actually geniuses. Maybe they understand and fully grasp that whole "being content in whatever state they are in" thing.

I needed reminding of that today, and I was happy to skip the run and sit on the wall with Roy to hear what he had to say.

By the way, we both enjoyed the chewing gum.

Look Closely

Well, what do we have here?

There was a time in my life that I would have said that you simply have four old guys posing for a camera. Now, I look at it as four extremely handsome gentlemen with over two hundred years of combined experience.

We've each witnessed the best and yes, at times, the absolute worst that life can throw at you. So many times, we've experienced those moments together.

It was a Friday afternoon and I was slowly awakening in a somewhat foreign world ...I so hope hospital beds never become commonplace. I was confused as I looked around the room trying to focus and process not just what was happening, but *what* had just happened. It was a room filled shoulder to shoulder with buddies of mine all looking at me as if they were cautiously awaiting my response. The fellow in the picture above on the far left? He was standing right beside my bed that afternoon as he leaned over and said just a few words. He spoke words that we have each repeated several times since ...words that I shall not repeat here. I can remember immediately laughing and it was almost like a jump-start to the next phase of my life. It was a very important laugh and the rest of the room was soon joining in with us. Yes, I so needed that laugh, but truthfully, I think we all needed it. He was the perfect friend, in the perfect spot to speak those first words to me. On that day, death had passed by, but thankfully chose not to stop. That afternoon, in that hospital room, was such a defining moment in my life and I was once again reminded that laughter and tears can be such a beautiful combination.

The fellow next to him? Twenty-five years ago, we had embarked on a career in advertising. Our days were spent laying out ads, writing copy and trying to figure out ways to land new business with very little experience and a portfolio that somehow was always mysteriously left at another client's office earlier in the day. We had landed an opportunity to pitch a client, a big client, one that could put us on the advertising map. Strangely, this opportunity began as a chance meeting and a simple conversation. Sure, that's not so strange, but this chance meeting and this conversation took place in the bathroom at the old Brass Register. Now, keep in mind, this was downtown Chattanooga in the 1980s. There was no Aquarium, no cool themed restaurants, beer choices were few and boy was advertising fun back then. Package design? Sure we could do that.

If folks back then only knew that while we were trying to convince them how good we were, we were also trying to convince ourselves as well. We spent days preparing for that meeting, a meeting with huge implications. That Friday morning, just hours before our eagerly anticipated appointment, things took a strange and somewhat unexpected turn. He would now have to drop by the office, put on the official wing tips, grab a tie out of the closet and fly solo on this one. Later that morning, he called me with these words ..."we got the account". Just a few minutes later, my son would be born. A big account ...a much bigger moment.

The guy to his left? Let's go back to the fall of 1985. A confident swagger that I had carried with me throughout that very day was suddenly replaced by uncontrollable gastric convulsions and an equally sudden loss of all sense of rational reasoning. The pews were packed and for some reason, they had each decided on their own to begin spinning in various patterns much like the Tilt-A-Whirl at Lake Winnepesaukah. By that time, I was quite sure all the blood that once gave my face color and that youthful glow of innocence, had decided to abandon me at this most important moment. Its absence leaving me with a pale and somewhat ashen-gray appearance, an appearance that I was most assured would place serious thoughts of doubt into my soon bride-to-be. Now, keep in mind, this was all taking place mere seconds before her exuberant entrance from the back of the church. Horrified, I turned to my left and there he was wearing a tux just like mine, smiling like a kid at a carnival. Somehow, I now felt some comfort. If I were to fall, maybe it would be in that direction, I just knew he would catch me. I leaned that way as the music began.

Yep, they've each been there during various milestone moments in my life. That's just what buddies do and you must trust me on this one, I could tell you many more stories.

So you see, I don't see four old guys in that picture. I simply see my life in one snapshot.

Sometimes, you just have to look closely.

That's What Earl Played

It was April of 1979.

I was twenty years old that night when me and some buddies strolled into Buckets O'Brien, a bar on Brainerd Road in Chattanooga, just to have a few beers. Bill McCallie and his band were tossing out some bluegrass tunes for everyone's listening and dancing pleasure. Sure, I had heard bluegrass for seemingly my entire life. Let's face it, who didn't watch Flatt and Scruggs on the Beverly Hillbillies?

Lester and Earl were the true rock stars of the bluegrass genre back in those days. They also had their own TV show that we would watch on Saturday afternoons. Ernest Tubb, Porter Wagner, the Wilburn Brothers ...they all had shows back then. Various country stars of the day would drop by and make appearances on these informal thirty-minute extensions of the old radio shows. One week you might get to see Loretta Lynn come out and give Ernest a hug. He'd give her a "bless your heart, honey" and then send her off to belt out her latest honky-tonk classic for us to enjoy. You just never knew from week to week who would be entering your living room: Faron Young, Charlie Louvin, Conway Twitty, Bobby Bare. Every Saturday we would get to see and hear folks that I had previously been introduced to through that single speaker in the back of Dad's Plymouth.

Wait just a second—I forgot to mention Dolly.

Hard-working, red-blooded southern men would gladly sit through Porter's latest hit, then a Speck Rhodes comedy routine, a Mack Magaha fiddle tune, a few words from our sponsors, Soltice and Black Draught cough syrup, another Speck Rhodes classic, and then back to a dramatic recitation song by Porter. Yes, they would sit patiently through each and every segment of the telecast just so they could get to the most important part of the show ...a chance to finally see and hear Dolly Parton. That woman could sing, and, bless her heart, she could write them songs about hard times in east Tennessee. She was a wonderful songstress. But, it was her presentation, if you will, that brought the men inside from various chores around the house. Dolly had a way of making the black and white and various gray tones on the televisions seem downright colorful to the menfolk.

My dad loved to watch ball games on our old rabbit-ear adorned television set. I learned how to adjust those ears just right for him soon after I took my very first steps on Carden Avenue. I learned to work the channel knob too. Looking back,

I guess I was Dad's first remote. I still believe to this day that Dolly is the real reason that my daddy worked extra hard to get us a color TV. I can still remember the afternoon it was delivered to our house, across from the pink house there in the valley. I'm sure we were the talk of both sides of that dirt road for several days.

It's years later now, and I'm sitting there with the guys at Buckets O'Brien. Honestly, we were there to drink beer, just another fun night with the guys; the music was like an unexpected appetizer ...but soon the music became the main course. I was seeing bluegrass music played up close and in person. It would change everything. I knew that very night that I wanted to play the banjo ...'cause that's what Earl played.

I headed out the very next day to Manny Bowen's music store at the old Eastgate Mall with my newly received income tax refund in hand, somewhere in the neighborhood of one hundred and twenty dollars. A deal was struck, and a part of my personal history was made. I was able to purchase a banjo, a case, picks, and an Earl Scruggs book, which contained a 45 record along with a "practice hard and good luck!" send off from Mr. Manny himself.

I went back home, basically locked myself in my bedroom, put that record on the ol' player, and began to listen and try desperately to figure out just what the heck Mr. Scruggs was doing. I worked and I worked, over and over ...I would even find myself practicing a three-finger roll on my leg as I was standing in line at the convenience store. I would come home from work or school, grab a bite, and then head back to my spot in front of that phonograph. Yes, I was obsessed, but you see, I knew that fame, fortune, and an endless buffet of girls awaited me if I could just perfect that mid-neck backup technique. You just know that Lester and Earl had to fight the women off after every show as they tried to climb back on their Martha White tour bus and head to their next gig.

Finally, three months later I emerged from my bedroom declaring myself a bona fide banjo player. Within a year I was in a band and thus began my professional bluegrass career. Now, I must say the fame and fortune were a little slower to come than I had hoped for, and also, to my surprise, not all girls were totally into the banjo like I had envisioned. That was OK ...I was in a band, man.

A couple of years later, our band was being booked regularly around the area, and I just knew we were maybe one break away from matching suits for the whole band when a buddy called to tell me that Earl was coming to town. Earl had formed a band with his sons called the Earl Scruggs Revue, and they were going to play at a venue down on the river just off Market Street. Tickets, we've got to get tickets. I would have immediately reached for the computer keyboard if only this marvelous tool of technological advancement wasn't still being worked on in a garage out in California.

Like a good chase scene from a Bond movie, we bolted through the streets of downtown Chattanooga that afternoon, dodging roadblocks and paying no attention to one-way signs. We got airborne as made that final turn and then slid in sideways into the parking lot. Jumping out of my Jeep, we dashed on foot the final few feet to the ticket office. Now, totally out of breath, but with cash in hand, we were able to purchase some great seats, thankfully beating the throng of fans that were sure to follow.

The night finally arrived, and we got there early. I watched the guys set up the sound equipment, and I saw his sons helping out ...but no Earl. Things were kind of quiet, so I excused myself for a trip to the restroom and another visit to the concession stand. It was calm before the storm time, and we had to be fully stocked ...locked and loaded if you will.

I can distinctly remember walking down a long hall. It kind of curved, and I saw a man walking slowly ahead of me ... He was wearing black pants, a white shirt and a black leather jacket. He opened a door to his right, which I knew headed out to the back. I walked faster and opened that door as well ...I looked out, and there was the bus, and this man was entering it ...I knew then I may very well be in the presence of greatness. I spoke, he turned around, and I found myself looking eye to eye with one of my all-time heroes ...Mr. Earl Scruggs. I would soon find out he was one of the most humble and gracious men I have ever met.

No entourage, no burly security guards, no throngs of autograph-seekers ...it was just me and Earl.

We spoke for a little while, he gave me his autograph, and he shook my hand. Yes, this was most certainly one of the highlights of my life. All these years later and that moment still plays in my mind very slowly, and it rings so true and clear like Earl punching the background notes to Lester's vocals.

Soon, he would take the stage and absolutely bring the proverbial house down. An absolute, 100-percent musical genius. You should have been there.

Later on in 1985, I purchased a 1929 Gibson Mastertone from Mr. George Gruhn in Nashville that I own to this day, 'cause that's what Earl played.

I am remembering that chance meeting this morning as I let the news of Earl Scruggs passing sink in. Please, make no mistake, in my opinion, Earl Scruggs was as important to music as Beethoven, Mozart, Elvis, the Beatles ...I could go on. Music became different because of his existence. Mr. Scruggs developed a three-finger style of picking a five-string banjo that is "often emulated, but never duplicated" around the world today. It is an absolutely distinctive sound of our American culture. He was buttery smooth, even in those last years. He was loved, he was respected, and those in the know were very aware that we had been in the presence of a true master ...the rarest of the rare.

I'll get my banjo out of its case and pick it proudly today, and I will remember Mr. Earl Scruggs. In fact, I'm thinking a little "Foggy Mountain Breakdown" would be appropriate about right now.

Dang, I still love that E minor.

Hard Times Come Again No More

My dad was a strong and tough man. He grew up in a time when that was how you survived. He lost his dad when he was around eleven years of age, a loss that left his mom with four hungry children to feed. These were the forties; times were always hard...but now they were going to get much harder.

He never talked about his dad much. I saw a picture of him one time, and I remember just a couple of stories he had offered to me. It was as if there was resentment over the fact that he was not among us. Looking back, I can see why my daddy never talked much about him. My grandfather was sick, bedridden-sick, for so long that there was never time to actually accumulate life memories, those special stories that we pass on to our kids. There simply were no stories.

He told me about the funeral one time. He remembered looking at the casket, and he felt an anger that his dad had left

DALE FORRESTER

them like that ..."How could you just leave us?" Those were his words ...leaving, as if it was a choice. Coping with a death is hard at any age, any age ...but an eleven-year-old should simply not have to face that event.

He never mentioned that day again.

My dad was an extremely talented man. Most folks never knew he had a wonderful singing voice. I used to hear it as we would ride down the road in his truck, and we rode in the truck a lot when I was a little kid. He could draw—oh my, could he draw; he could draw most anything. He was one of the funniest people I ever knew, and he could tell the most wonderful stories. He could paint portraits, he could write ...in some ways, talent absolutely oozed out of his pores.

You can't pursue it though ...you've got to work. You can't accept that small, partial scholarship to Georgia Tech, 'cause there was simply no way to make up the difference ...you've got to work. Life is hard, and the sooner you get started with that hard life, the better. That's just the way it was.

Construction was a way for him to begin his climb.

My dad worked so hard for so many years until finally he started his own construction company. I can remember he was always stressed, always worrying about the weather—the cold, the rain—it seemed there was always concrete to be poured. He seemingly had no peace at times. He just couldn't stop.

As I hit my mid-teen years and the mention of the word *future* began to be tossed around, I just figured I would go into construction ...after all, it was the family business. The very mention of that drew an immediate, gentle, but very stern

156

response from my dad ...he absolutely was not going to allow that to occur.

Looking back now, I can see what was happening. He had taught me nothing about the craftsmanship of construction; he instead introduced me—and not very gently, mind you—to the absolute backbreaking end of it.

From the time I was sixteen, I would work for Daddy during various breaks from school and through the summer. Wheelbarrow, sledgehammer, shovel, lifting, and lifting some more. He would work me until I would collapse when I finally got to go home that night. My only reprieve was during the summer months when I would have a baseball game—he would back off on me a little after lunch.

At night, I would sleep like a baby, and I often prayed for rain so maybe, just maybe, I could have a day off. God never helped me with that one.

Now, about the picture. It's the summer of 1975 ...I'm sixteen years old and skinny, but finally my growth spurt had begun. My dad is building a new bank just across the state line into Tennessee. I was working one day, doing my usual grunt work, when he came to me with a project that needed to be done. I was more than happy to get away from that shovel and wheelbarrow, and somehow I felt important. Obviously my dad had recognized and needed my special set of skills, whatever they may be.

I can remember us standing on the northern curbside of the property, and he started giving me my instructions. He needed the asphalt dug up about three feet from the curb, all the way from Rossville Boulevard up to Dodds Avenue. It looked like a mile to me at the time. The tool for this ambitious project would be a jackhammer. Now, I had never operated a jackhammer before, but I was quite sure I could master this difficult instrument. I soon would find out that the jackhammer weighed more than my one hundred and forty pound frame, and a three-inch bit would make the job even more challenging.

For three solid days, I worked that jackhammer. Pounding and pounding at times until it would make my whole body itch from the jarring vibrations. I used every ounce of strength I could possibly muster to lift it up and set that three-inch bit back into the extremely hot asphalt ...July in the South. I started at the corner on Rossville Boulevard and simply never looked up. I can still remember my arms feeling as if they weren't there. I was getting light-headed and thinking at times I simply couldn't lift this thing anymore. Thankfully my dad's "gentle" persuasion at times would convince me otherwise.

I felt I simply could not please him.

At the end of that third day, I had made it all the way to Dodds Avenue. I had separated the asphalt three feet away from the curb, three inches at a time for twenty-four grueling work hours. Physically, it was the hardest three days of my life ...exactly what my dad would want me to remember thirty-some odd years later. Sure, he could have rented a piece of equipment to do that project in a couple of hours, but instead he chose his son—the son that he refused to let enter the family business—because he never wanted him on a jackhammer again.

It worked.

Today I drove by that old building, and I looked over at that side street, and amazingly the asphalt that was used to cover up my work is still there—you can see the darker asphalt all the way to Dodds.

My dad made sure that I was able to pursue my dreams... dreams that life somewhat denied him.

He deserved better, and I think about that all the time.

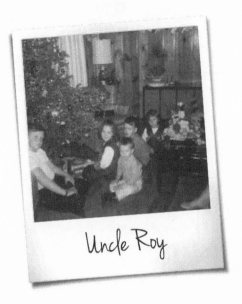

Uncle Roy

We buried my uncle Roy yesterday.

Roy has this dominant place in my childhood memories as if he had always been there, you know, like always. That's why I was shocked when the preacher told us he was seventy-eight years old. I just had never actually placed a date on the beginning of his existence.

Roy had the single most humble and jovial spirit that was ever placed upon a man. He was simply always laughing. A gentle laugh, never dominating a room. He made this little kid want to be at his house anytime I could, and that was very often.

At the end of Clara Lee Drive, I could play with my hero, my cousin Chuck. We'd play out in the yard with GI Joes, maybe throw a football around, and then come back in all scuffed up to eat my aunt Gaynelle's cooking. Then we'd lie on the

161

floor and talk about little boy stuff and giggle while Jim Reeves records played in the background. I still can remember those beautiful wood-paneled walls wrapping the living room and the warmth of the golden lights as they softly bounced off them ...and Roy laughing.

Saturday mornings we'd wake up early and lie on that same living room floor under Pinkie and Blue Boy and watch Roy Rogers on WRCB-TV. Roy would be in his chair at the opposite end of the room, reading the newspaper and wearing a white T-shirt, along with a face that was simply made by God for a smile.

So, I'm thinking about Roy on this rainy Saturday morning, the day after his funeral. I got up early this morning and began looking for a picture of him in some old photo albums. Sadly, I don't own a really good one of just him. Sure, I could make a call and get one, but I then came across a picture of five little kids sitting in the floor ...my cousin Chuck to the left and cousins Lisa, Tammy, Kenny, and myself sitting under the glow of those wood-paneled walls at Christmas. Roy would like this; yep, I can feel him laughing now.

I will choose this picture to remember him today.

It's amazing when you look back on childhood the things that you remember. I have these simple memories placed in a safe box and stored in my mind. My good memories are so easily accessible. I bring them out at times to enjoy them, and I always put them neatly back in their place. Those are my treasures and are to be treated with the utmost of care.

We said good-bye yesterday, but it's just for a little while. At the end, as folks left that room one by one after paying their final respects, I made sure to lag behind. I didn't shed a tear. I stood there, I closed my eyes, and I reached back into my mind and opened that box, and there he was. He was sitting in his chair, smiling, and I smiled too. I then placed Roy neatly back into my mind's treasure box, opened my eyes, and enjoyed the rest of the day with my family.

God doesn't place the Roys of this world here by accident. They have a spirit that we need, and thankfully Roy had thoughtfully passed that same spirit on to his son, my cousin Chuck.

And though I tried with all of my sadness,
somehow I could never weep
for a man who looked to me
like he died laughing in his sleep.
"Play a Train Song" by Todd Snider

We will see you again, uncle Roy. RTR.

Hot Dogs, Cold Night

I can't tell you the exact year, but my best guess would be around November or December of 1978. I can tell you it was an extremely cold night at the end of a cold day. It was that early-season cold that sometimes reaches a little deeper into your bones as if to shake you and remind you of what's coming in the weeks and months ahead.

I say 1978 because I know I was out of high school, and my best friend, Robbie, had that black CJ-5 Jeep. He was the first of our gang to get a Jeep, and it set off a trend that would continue upward of seven deep in the crowd that I ran with. This was back when Jeeps were manly machines consisting of plain old American metal ...no plastic anywhere, including the dash and glove compartment (that's for another story). If you wanted to maneuver around in four-wheel drive, then somebody's gonna have to get out into the elements, often times mud, and "lock the hubs." Those Jeeps ran on gas, oil, and testosterone. Tanks whimpered at their very sight. In fact, those old CJs are the only vehicles I've ever known that sported a three-day growth.

Now, some of my earliest thespian experiences occurred during some of these various, quite memorable jaunts. Trying to act tough requires a certain talent and concentration level—a level of believability that even convinces yourself that you can whoop that somewhat imposing fellow across the room if need be, or down just one more cold beer. Looking back, I believe I convinced only myself with my acting abilities.

That night we pulled into the market at the corner of Mission Ridge and McFarland to buy some supplies before we headed up onto the ridge. Between the two of us, we had just enough money—which would have included the contents of both our billfolds and any and all loose change we could scrounge up—to buy some hot dog buns, some weenies, mustard, ketchup, chips, a couple of candy bars, some Little Debbies, and perhaps a six-pack of Coke. That sounds like a lovely night of campfire cuisine.

Or, we had another option.

We also had just enough money to buy a couple of Miller Pony eight-packs, a loaf of bread, and some weenies. No mustard, no ketchup, no chips, no fancy hot dog buns, no candy bars, no Little Debbies, and no Cokes. Quaint and somewhat simple fare I must say.

That night we were of the belief that simpler was indeed better.

We made our purchases posthaste and headed down Hogan Road just past the Peach Orchards to the narrow, somewhat hidden red dirt entrance on the left. We got out and locked the hubs in preparation for the winding and rough trek up the ridge side high atop South Crest overlooking the rock crusher and the old barn down in the valley below us. Soon, we would count stars, talk about baseball, a little about girls, and try to stay as close to the fire as possible—that temperature would most assuredly keep on dropping.

You just know the old pioneers spent nights like this.

We finally reached the summit, shall we say, and I am most assured that the temperature up there was a good two to three degrees lower than what we were experiencing no more than just five minutes ago. We were roughing it like Yukon skin traders, and now it was time to gather the essentials to build a fire.

Soon, we had sticks and paper and wood a-blazing ...the flames giving everything they touched that soft glow of amber that warms the heart long before it warms the fingers and toes. I never knew a girl who didn't look even more lovely sitting by that glow. To this day, I love the feel, the sound, and the smell of a campfire. Why, oh why, don't I build one more often?

We trimmed a couple of limbs to use as primitive weenie cooking utensils. I could almost picture Daniel Boone having one of these exact moments. Maybe he didn't use Oscar Mayer ...but still. I watched my perfectly crafted stick carefully as I slid it between the warm yellow and orange hues. Through years of experience, I had learned that the trick is to see the weenie just about to get black and then, at that exact moment, take it out and let the cooking process finish away from the fire. My timing this night was once again exquisite. I placed the perfectly prepared weenie on a piece of white bread and then sat down with a frigid Pony, just like the cowboys used to do out on the prairie in the old Wild West days. Robbie was already kicked back and ready to enjoy his delicacy as well.

It is at this exact point of the story that a simple cold night around a campfire became legendary ...a moment that will surely be passed down for generations to come.

I took a bite and suddenly it was as if I was hearing applause and joyous tears from the heavens as the soundtrack for the night changed from Lynyrd Skynyrd to the London Philharmonic. When I was finally able to gather myself, I looked across the fire toward Robbie and noticed his eyes were closed—or perhaps they had rolled into the back of his head—as a smile slowly grew, soon encompassing his entire face. It was most evident to me that he was having the same majestic moment that I had just had. He opened his tear-filled eyes slowly and looked toward me. We knew exactly right then and there that these truly were the best hot dogs we had ever eaten, and not just that, but perhaps these were the best hot dogs there had ever been. Simply a weenie, a slice of white bread, and an ice-cold beer.

That night Robbie slept by the fire, and I somehow slept curled up like a bloodhound in the back of the Jeep covered with my coat as the temperatures continued to drop. I can specifically remember that next morning. We were greeted with an extremely damp fog and a brutal coldness that was remedied rather quickly with the heat from inside the CJ-5. Make no mistake about it—those old Jeep heaters could thaw a frozen turkey in three minutes tops.

On that early morning on the way back down the ridge to Hogan Road, we finally worked up the courage to talk about what had just happened. We spoke slowly and in hushed tones. How could that have been the best hot dog we ever had? It was just a weenie and a piece of white bread, for goodness' sake ...how did that happen? Should we contact the media? No, we concluded, they would never believe us ...kinda like those mountain folks who see UFOs from time to time.

To this day, I simply cannot explain it. All I can say is this: on a night that the winter air could take your breath from you if it so desired, sitting by a popping, crackling, and glowing fire that climbed upward above the trees and on toward the clouds, under a covering of stars that seemingly blanketed us and all the valley below, Robbie and I had a special dinner ...a special moment. A moment that thirty-some odd years later, we still bring up from time to time and speak of with the exact same awe we did that night.

We're still trying to find one better.

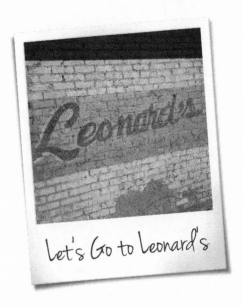

Let's Go to Leonard's

It was probably when I was around fifteen years old or so, you know, that awkward time when you're just starting to grow up. You're too young for the high school girls, and you think you're too old for the junior high girls. Video games weren't around, no cell phones, no Internet, no interest in TV. I was just a little kid who wanted to be one of the big guys. All I worried about was baseball, trying to fit in, and why my voice was starting to crack all the time.

Then I got to go to Leonard's.

Leonard's was a bar near the tunnels on Brainerd Road in Chattanooga. I got invited to go with some of the big guys, which for me was kind of like getting called up to the majors, even if it was just for one game. I can still remember walking in and trying to stand taller. My growth spurt would not start until the next year. These were the days before serious carding took place ...the pre-"Just Say No" days.

We all sat at a big, rough-hewed table, and soon a couple of pitchers full of beer arrived. Truthfully, I had never seen a pitcher in real life, and I'm sure I was possibly studying it as all the other guys were ordering the famous Leonard's burger. When my turn came, I confidently ordered one too ...as if that was my usual.

There I sat with my mug full of beer, laughing with the guys and trying to act older than I really was. I found myself being extra careful of any move I made or possible interjection I added to the conversation. I was trying to fit in, and I was keenly aware that I could be sent back to the minors with one mistake or garner an unflattering nickname that would stick with me for life if I were to somehow embarrass myself. Luckily, I didn't have to concern myself with decisions such as which utensil to use first. Belching was OK, and if my elbows were to somehow end up on the table, I do not believe it would have been counted against me.

Then the Leonard's burger arrived.

Trust me, it was bigger than the plate ...in fact; it more resembled the size of a large pizza. It was so big that to this day when I see a hubcap, I think of Leonard's. Looking back, I think even the pickles were big, and I'm sure you could haven eaten the sesame seeds like salted peanuts. To this very day, I have never seen a burger that size.

Here I was, having one of those *Wonder Years* moments. I ~~drank a beer~~ tried to drink a beer, ate most of this beefy monstrosity, and just soaked everything in. Yep, I was one of the guys, one of the big guys. This was my rite of passage ...my very own southern, good ol' boy Bar Mitzvah if you will. From then on, I thought of myself differently.

Leonard's has been closed for years now, and honestly, I hadn't thought about it in some time until a buddy called me this morning to tell me that the old sign is still visible on the outside wall out back. I just had to see it for myself. So, I dropped by this afternoon to pay a visit. There it was in all its glory ...a piece of my younger days that I hadn't seen in well over thirty years.

Now, I'm not one of those who think all the best times happened when I was young. In my opinion, if that's the case, then you have really wasted a large portion of your life. Truth is, being young can be really hard—trying to fit in, having your heart absolutely broken and crushed—but sometimes, I think back to moments like this one, and I so want to go back.

Well, just for a little while.

Five Strings
and Angel's Wings

It was April of 1985, and my lifelong buddy Danny and I left out early to make our usual once-a-month Saturday pilgrimage to Gruhn's in Nashville. The old Gruhn's music store was a narrow, shotgun-style building there on Broadway, just a few doors down from Tootsie's. Now, this was back in the day when an early-Saturday morning walk up that street meant stepping over a few drunks and possibly passing by one of the ladies from the night before still trying to practice her craft. Things have most definitely changed in that part of town since those days.

We would make this journey up to Nashville to simply hang out and listen to and sometimes pick with some of the very best musicians around in one of the back rooms. You see, Mr. Gruhn had the finest collection of vintage acoustic instruments in the world (even more so today), and he would let you take most anything off the wall you wanted and find you a room, where you could play, oftentimes with studio-caliber musicians, for as long as you liked. It was our own personal Disney World, and I still have a warm spot for that place.

We would usually pick until around 2:00 and then make the two-hour drive back down to our regular gig at JB's just across the river, off north Market in Chattanooga. Ah, the days of being a "professional" bluegrass musician.

But this day was going to be a little different.

We found us a parking spot there on Third Avenue and strolled on down toward Broadway. We made our way up the sidewalk, past the locals, and finally to the entrance. As we reached for the door, I looked to my left, and there it was ...it startled me at first. Behind the large glass window covered with jail bars sat several instruments on music stands and one very important one ...a vintage Gibson Mastertone banjo. I didn't have to be told, I just knew.

You see, back in the day, if you had a Gibson Mastertone made before WWII, you were special. It automatically raised your musician standing in the community at least two notches, possibly even three. People would suddenly speak of you with awe and reverence.

For the previous several years, I had carried a check with me every single time I visited Nashville for this exact reason. You just never knew. This could be the day ...the day the blue-grass gods would place a pre-war Gibson within my grasp, so I had to be prepared.

I remember walking in, already nervous as I asked to see it. I held it in many ways like you hold a newborn. You know the feeling—it's as if you've never held anything before, and you're not totally sure what to do with your hands. You're holding a gift to the world, and you must not let harm come to this precious creature.

Time was about to place itself on hold for a while. Danny had grabbed an old Martin, and we were suddenly in a room with three or four other guys. We were picking, and the angels were dancing and singing, and I could not picture a sound more beautiful.

I would eventually emerge from that back room sometime later only to realize that it was around 1:00 p.m. Somehow three hours had disappeared.

I somewhat anxiously approached Mr. Gruhn about the banjo. It was a nervous kind of feeling, like meeting the parents for the first time. He then gave me the particulars about the instrument. It was a 1929 Gibson Mastertone TB-3, and it belonged to Larry McNeely ...a very well-respected musician in Nashville. Larry had played with Glen Campbell, Roy Acuff, and the Smothers Brothers, among others, *and* he had supplied the background music for the *Dukes of Hazzard* on this particular banjo. He was selling several of his instruments to help finance a cabin he was building nearby.

I do remember finally asking for the price. When he tossed it at me, I didn't even wince, although by my standards, it was a rather hefty sum. It was more than I had ever spent on anything in my life other than my car ...but I just had to have it.

177

(One more important tidbit: I was getting married that fall, and I was very keenly aware that I had a possible "now or never" situation on my hands.)

I chose to go with now.

I reached into my wallet and produced my check, my only check, and nervously started writing ...very slowly. My hands were shaking and sweaty and yes, wouldn't you just know it, I messed the check up. I immediately began hyperventilating, and my first thought was to tell him to "hold on, I'll be right back" ...of course, this meant a two-plus hour drive each way back to the house to get another check. That's when logic somehow introduced itself to me, and using a check I borrowed from Danny, I was able to complete this historic transaction.

My mother would later say that she knew it must be some more banjo, "'cause it takes him six months to pick out a pair of shoes."

A few months later I would be married, and of course, my Gibson was a groomsman and remains an important, although a very much neglected, member of the family now to this very day.

I used to play almost around the clock for years, but now, I rarely ever get it out of the case. I guess my life goes in chapters, and obviously, it seems, that chapter was closed years ago.

Sad? Just a bit melancholy? Nah. Let's face it, if I had to play "Rocky Top" one more time, I think I'd just have to go ahead and shoot someone.

Trust me, in certain parts of the South, that crime would be perfectly understood and excusable.

The Saint of Salem Road

He was an electrician by trade, a retired electrician from Yates Bleachery over in the valley, just a few miles across the state line from Chattanooga. He had a tattoo on his right forearm as I recall ...a tattoo that looked like the artist had possibly spilled his ink bottle and then simply had tried to blot it off. I never did know exactly what it was. It was possibly a pirate or maybe it was an eagle. He wore glasses, glasses that actually used to belong to my great-grandpa, my granny's dad. His name was Paul, Paul Catlett.

Now, I am the grandson of Paul Forrester. He was the father of my dad, my uncle and two aunts. My grandfather Paul died twelve years before I came along. Then, five years or so later, my granny would remarry. She took as her husband a lanky man, with a comfortable disposition ...this other Paul, whom we all knew simply as Pap.

When I think of Pap, and luckily I do very often, I think of Salem Road, lots of thick hair with very little gray and building tent forts in their little frame house up on that hill using dining room chairs and a sheet. I think of a man sitting beside the hospital bed of my Granny patting her arm and talking softly and sweetly to her as she lay there recovering from a near fatal auto accident in that bad curve at Happy Valley Farms. I see a man smiling from his recliner by the picture window as grand-kids excitedly scrambled around the floor of that house on the hill opening presents on another cozy Christmas Eve ...a coziness I have been totally unable to recreate all these years and I so desperately ache for it at times. I see a man whose very demeanor was so kind and gentle that I have used him as the benchmark to define a good grandpa all throughout my life. I see a man who could fix most anything, loved his wife's BBQ chicken and his Bible, was sparse with words, smiled often and always had some black electrical tape. I see a man who made much with very little. A man who loved sardines and potted meat, Ernest Tubb and listening to his police scanner. I see a man who married into a situation that had to be tough and helped finish raising four kids as if they were his very own, kids that worshiped him all his days. I also see a man who would later on, after his death, be promoted to sainthood by those same little kids who used to crawl around the floor giggling amongst the multicolored wrapping paper and shiny bows.

I also see a man who loved to fish.

Now, when you worked at Yates Bleachery, one part of your benefits package was unlimited use of the Yates Ponds which sat nestled at the base of Lookout Mountain, about seven to eight miles or so south of the mill, down past the High Point community. The entrance was beside a little house on your right as you topped a hill on that long and curvy two-lane stretch of highway. A little house that sits to this day all to its lonesome with a train track nestled between kudzu-covered hills and thick trees a hundred feet or so across the street and the mountains resting outside the back door. Pull into the dirt driveway, unlatch the gate and then walk on down a winding one lane dirt road. Soon, you will come upon the first of, to the best of my memory, seven ponds. Each crystal pool reflects the blue skies and puffy clouds that seem to enjoy this mirror that He gave them. They lay there all quiet and still, protected with care by the constant presence of Lookout Mountain. A mountain that has seemed to frame so much of my life.

So exclusive are these grounds that some people in the area simply do not know of their existence. In fact, most folks will live their entire lives around here without once getting the chance to gaze at what an eight year old boy first captured in his mind all those years ago. A place that I can still describe to you today. A place I have not visited in well over forty years.

These are privileged and sacred waters my friend. These natural and hidden collections of water known as Yates Ponds.

Several times, I got to go fishing at the ponds with Pap. I'd spend the night, sleeping in one of his old t-shirts that covered my knees as I slowly dozed off in the security of my tent fort. The next morning we'd wake before the sun, grab some biscuits Granny had just made for us, hop into that '64 Buick and head on out for our adventure. I figured that fish must wake up real early too.

As we made our way down through the valley, the sun would slowly begin to appear ...a sight that my eyes were simply not accustomed to viewing, at least not from that direction or at that particular time of day. Soft pastels from the red and yellow spectrum marked its peaceful arrival, and I thought that surely it was yawning too as my head rested up against the glass on the passengers side ...the hum of the engine softly encouraging me to finish the rest of my nap that had been taken from me so abruptly. I would doze in and out just hoping it took a long time to get there. The country hits of the day entertained us on that crackly AM radio, its static often keeping the beat through that one lonesome speaker.

Finally, the trail would end ...the crunching noise of tires against rocks signaling our arrival. I'd stretch and groan with everything in me trying to get that last bit of sleepiness out of my body the best I could. We'd hop out, grab our fishing stuff, unlatch the gate and make the final part of the trek on foot down the path, around a bend, finally reaching that first pond.

We would fish with worms or sometimes crickets we bought from the hatchery the day before over on Wilson Road. We also fished with a float as God, I am most assured, intended. Later on in life, as I started studying my Bible and began to learn more about the apostles, I became convinced that is the way they fished too. I just know it's in there. They were obedient, God-fearing, worm fishermen, except that sorry Judas Iscariot who you just know tossed the float aside and fished with the fanciest of lures and the most expensive rods to be found.

There's one in every crowd.

I still remember watching Pap's patient hands applying the bait onto the hook and explaining to me slowly what he was doing. Everything he did was somewhat slow, deliberate you might say. Truthfully, there was no wasted motion and the words he spoke flowed in the same exact manner. I so wish I had carried a notebook and made some notes.

Now, I'd like to be able to tell you how much I loved fishing back then, but I would be lying. It bored me …it really did. I was just a little single-digit kid, eight years old at the most when we started going. Like most any little boy, I had no attention span, and I could be distracted easily by the least crackle of a leaf or a Brown Thrasher piercing the air with its sweet songs. To sit for long periods of time and watch a float was hard for me. But, I was with Pap and it somehow made me feel like a big boy.

Truthfully, all these years later and I still haven't acquired one of those spans. I used to think of it as a flaw, but I'm not so sure anymore.

I do so remember the thrill of watching that float go under and tugging madly trying to set the hook. That moment of excitement as I fought and fought to reel in my prize. I can remember Pap grabbing a hold of it's slimy frame and showing me how to gently extract the hook from its mouth and release it back into the water. I would pet it gently in absolute amazement and admire its scales as the sun bounced off them releasing colors I had never seen before. A stroke on its head and then back to the water it would go. There was a respect for the fish, just as much as he respected the crystal waters we were fishing on.

Looking back, we never, ever caught many fish ...I can remember no more than three or so anytime we went. I also remember this, if we caught three, I would catch two ....if only one was caught, you just know who caught it. I would always be so excited and couldn't wait to get back to that house on the hill and tell Granny. She'd be so happy and surprised and would make over me when we walked in the back door and into her kitchen. Then we'd all sit there for the longest and eat a sandwich and talk about how in the world I was able to catch the most fish again. Pap would just grin, shake his head and brag about what a fine fisherman I was.

I guess you could say I was just a natural.

Do Not Seek the Sauce

I woke up around 5:00 a.m. the other morning from our stay at the historic Irma's in picturesque Cody, Wyoming. Randy and Larry and I were smack-dab in the middle of the greatest road trip there has ever been since they began documenting such adventures. I decided to take a shower and head on out for a little walk around town before breakfast.

After completing my early-morning tour of the town, I moseyed back to the dining room to meet the guys ...that's right, I moseyed, that's what we do out West. We proceeded to dine on the breakfast buffet, which I'm here to tell you was a huge spread. We ate too much, but we needed the extra carbs for fighting Indians and chasing down buffaloes, plus we needed to go to the Wal-Mart again.

Things were going just fine. It was a lovely, uneventful morning until our sweet waitress felt the obligation to remind us about their somewhat famous bread pudding dessert. Dessert for breakfast? Again, we needed some more carbs.

Accepting this kind invitation, Larry moseys back up to the buffet first—sorry, we found ourselves moseying a lot. He proceeds to spoon out a huge slab of said bread pudding, and it was at this very moment that our story takes an unsuspecting twist. The owner, a wiry, older fellow who would give most any room a sense of character by way of his very presence, says this: "Get ya some of that whiskey sauce." Now, a very large bowl of this specially created delicacy had been strategically placed right next to the huge tray of bread pudding. Larry, being a good southern boy, does what he's told, plus I'm sure he felt personally challenged. He proceeds to ladle on several spoonfuls of that special whiskey sauce and then strolled back to the table. OK, you guessed it, he actually moseyed once again.

Randy and I were immersed an in-depth discussion of worldly matters, at least that's the way I remember it, as Larry took his place back at our table, ready to enjoy this highly acclaimed breakfast delicacy.

The conversation continued, and I distinctly recall making an important point when I heard this loud steam-train whistle blow. Randy heard it too. I had gathered my thoughts to continue when the train announced its presence once again. It was at this moment that I turned slowly to my left to notice that thankfully it wasn't a train, but instead an obviously distressed and crimson-faced Larry. He was fumbling around, about to lose control of all bodily functions, and I was thinking I may finally get to break out that Heimlich maneuver I learned back in lifeguard training school. I would soon find out that he was desperately seeking some sort of liquid ...water, coffee, heck, Tabasco sauce ...anything to calm his innards. His eyes were all teary as they were about to roll back into his head, his face was now the color of cherry juice, and he couldn't readily speak. Randy had a panicked look, and I was trying to dial 911 when finally Larry murmured in a soft falsetto, "Watch out for the whiskey sauce."

As Larry goes for a somewhat smaller bite, I felt a curiosity, dare I say, an obligation to try this special dessert as well.

When I returned to the table, Larry was trying to do like his mama taught him and clean his plate of this mountainous, alcohol-drenched confection. As for yours truly, I had taken the cue and placed a somewhat smaller portion with only a tablespoon of the sauce on my plate. After one very cautious bite, I immediately realized that Larry would most certainly not be driving the morning shift of the next leg of our journey. In fact, after finishing that slab, he most likely would fail any breathalyzer in the state. It seems that our good friend Larry had just downed a huge slab of bread pudding thoroughly soaked with straight 180-proof whiskey.

Now, the preparation of the special whiskey sauce at Irma's is a somewhat simple three-step process, and in case you can't find it on Pinterest, I'll help you out.

1. Find the whiskey.
2. Remove cork from said whiskey bottle.
3. Pour contents into a bowl.

You've been warned. The bread pudding at Irma's: a two-drink minimum on a plate.

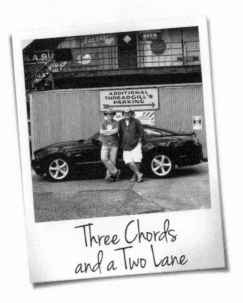

Three Chords and a Two Lane

I just got home from an ambush of the great state of Texas, and I'm sitting here at the house just trying to think back on the moments over the past week and catalog them in my mind for future reference.

A visit to Austin and the Longhorn State has long been a dream of mine since I really got into music right out of high school. I became fascinated with Texas initially by way of *Austin City Limits*. It would air every Saturday night at 7:00 on PBS, and on more than once occasion, I was mysteriously late for a date.

Willie Nelson, Waylon Jennings, Gary P. Nunn, Jerry Jeff Walker, Townes Van Zandt, and Guy Clark—their style of writing was unlike anything I had ever heard. It was storytelling by absolute masters who used fiddles and steel guitars for the soundtrack of their adventures. Later on I would add Lyle

Lovett and Robert Earl Keen to my playlist and in recent years, Bruce Robison, Charlie Robison, and Pat Green.

My heroes could write these songs that would take me to beautiful places in my mind. Places that I just knew existed, places that I so desperately wanted to see. They would strum three-chord stories that could bring you to tears or make you ache for a lost love. Tales of a longing for the simple life, or a perfectly arranged collection of words and musical notes, could magically carry you to fits of laughter. Wonderful adventures accented with a prickling of your emotions and often taken on dirt roads so real you could feel it on your skin. Journeys often sprinkled with seemingly endless honky-tonks, each amply supplied with ice-cold longnecks, wood floors, and "the friendliest people and the prettiest women you've ever seen." You could see it all through the windshield of a pickup truck.

Kindly, at the end, they would drop you back gently to the very place where the trip had started a mere four minutes ago. Just how could they do all of that in roughly two hundred and forty seconds?

There was so much truth and realness in the music. It seemed genuine and not the typical babble that Nashville so often places on the radio dial. Each of these guys had their own unique style of crafting words and presentation, but there was one universal tie ...an undying, deep sense of love and pride for their dear homeland of Texas.

I fell in love with a place I had never really been to. My closest visit was a trip in 1975 to Texarkana to play baseball, then, a few years ago, I ended up in the Dallas airport. But those simply didn't count. I had never really been to Texas.

Now I have.

Through simple existence, I have passed this love of music on to my son Corey ...he truly "gets it." He has introduced me to other singer/songwriters, and he has become an aficionado of Mr. Robert Earl Keen. In fact, he knows the words and the stories behind just about every single one of the one hundred thousand epics REK has penned. He also tosses in John Prine and Todd Snider, who, though not from Texas, have the same storytelling style.

My son and I don't see the world in the exact same way, and after years of frustration and at times great anger, I have learned this absolute truth that I would like to pass along at this time:

It's OK.

My son and I have found this one common ground where we are absolutely mirror images of one another.

I have been blessed to stick around long enough to realize this and to fulfill a dream, and I got to fulfill it with my son by my side. My gosh, my dream was his dream too.

Simply put, there isn't a father on this planet who wouldn't have wanted to be in my shoes.

God bless Texas.

Goodnight Sweet Lilly

Hers was somewhat less than a happy childhood.

Actually, she was born to be a show dog, a standard poodle that carried herself not only with style and grace, but her regal gait would sometimes stop strangers right there in their tracks as they gazed at her in wonderment. A childlike smile would then most assuredly encompass their faces as they viewed the loveliness she carried so naturally. Yep, she was born to show off the beauty and uniqueness of her breed, but for some reason the experts felt she didn't quite measure up. She had a flaw and would never be good enough.

I spent the last nine years trying to find that flaw, and for the life of me, I never found it.

Lillian spent her first couple of years relegated to life in a kennel. She was never groomed, and she was fed with all the other dogs at a communal trough once a night. How she came to live with us is a story unto itself. She arrived that night with long, matted hair and fear in her eyes, and she was completely void of the concept of love.

She took to me immediately and thus began our lifelong bond.

The next day, she made her first trip to the groomer, and that was when the magic happened. This disheveled mess of a dog was suddenly transformed into the single most beautiful dog I have ever seen ...my sweet Lilly. I so wish I had a before and after picture to share, but that was just another one of her eccentricities. She hated cameras.

I can't say she became an immediate member of the family. Truthfully, Lillian only opened up to me, and this would go on for upward of a year. She was timid and shy, and it was as if she lacked social skills. She would get up and exit a room each and every time my wife entered. For some reason, I was her life, her one and only. Yes, it was odd the way she would not allow herself to look past me and join the family ranks.

Then came Brie.

Brie was a six-week-old Bichon Frisé that we brought into our home only because Lillian was not interested in being the family dog. We knew about Brie before she was even born on that Valentine's Day at a friend's house a few miles away. My wife picked her out just a day or two after she was born and would visit her over the weeks until that day she could take her home. From the very moment those soft little paws hit the hardwood at 226, she was the perfect little dog. She took to playing with the whole family, including Lillian, but we all knew without a doubt she was a mama's dog. She had a personality much larger than her frame, and this little cotton ball puppy, in essence, brought Lilly out and introduced her to the rest of the world.

I can't explain it; it just happened.

Lillian soon became the happiest standard poodle you ever saw. She would jump and play and bark in the yard and act like the puppy that she probably never got to be. Brie was the alpha dog, and Lillian worshipped her. They played together, slept together, and did their business outside together. Lillian's transformation was sudden and absolute. She loved the entire family from then on.

Lilly was a nose poker, a trait that she used not only to get your attention but to show her love as well. She would always thank you for feeding her, and that nose would also let you know when she needed to use the outdoor facilities, or maybe when she just wanted you to stop and acknowledge her.

She loved doggie biscuits, the futon up in my man cave/office, Jeep rides, and oh how she loved for the wind to blow her ears. She would throw her head back and soak it all in. She absolutely did not have a mean bone in her entire fifty-two-pound body.

One night, Lilly and I were driving through the back roads of south Alabama, alone, when hunger pains and the empty light on the gas gauge told us we needed to find a place for a pit stop.

I found a lonely gas station on an even lonelier road that luckily had a Subway attached to it. I jumped out, placed the nozzle in the ol' truck, and it was then that Lillian gave me that look ...she needed some relief. I reached for her leash and began talking baby talk to her. I did that on a constant basis, and she not only loved it, but also kinda expected it from me.

We skipped on over to the vacant lot next door, and Lillian did her business. As usual after one of these events, she started jumping around like a puppy and barking like an alto, while I talked more mushy talk to her. We were having the best time. We so loved those moments.

As we made our way back, it was then I noticed three "good ol' boys" on the other side of the pumps by a rusted-out white Ford pickup. It was quite obvious they had been watching us play and most likely had heard me talking sweetly to my girl.

Yep, we had ourselves the makings of a possible hate crime about to happen here in rural south Alabama ...a perfect story-line for the boys on *Law & Order*, and you just know that CNN would have crawled all over it.

"What kinda dog is that?" one of them inquired, as he slowly looked her over. I confidently stood my ground and told him she was a standard poodle. Honestly, I didn't know what to expect next, as Lillian looked back at them with the confidence of a Westminster champ. I know it's hard to look strong and confident when you're sitting there sporting cute little pink flowery ribbons adorning your lovely groomed and fluffy ears, but she was pulling it off. For just a split second, I swear it felt like one of those showdown scenes right out of *Tombstone*.

OK, I know Wyatt Earp probably never saw a poodle in his life, but work with me here.

It was almost time to reach for our holsters, when suddenly he began to melt, and as God is my witness, the other two guys were smiling and giggling along with him. They were viewing something they had never seen before, and Lillian started pouring on the charm. They each started rubbing the top of her head and laughing like a bunch of little sixth-graders on the playground.

Trust me on this one—southern Alabama boys appreciate beauty and class just as much as the rest of this world. Yep, they knew how to talk baby talk too ...even the toughest of men couldn't resist sweet Lillian. Shame on me for thinking otherwise.

She and I split a foot-long Italian Marinara sandwich that night and laughed about making some new friends as we headed on up the road. She loved good food ...I guess it was the French in her.

Lillian and I often slept together. She stayed with me while I worked, she huddled up close to me during thunderstorms, and she cried for me when I was gone.

Tonight I cried, because now she's gone, and I do not know when these tears will stop.

Ironically, this past week I was on Facebook and came across a piece that a friend of mine had commented on. It was a piece written by a friend of his about the very subject of dogs not going to heaven ...I read it completely from top to bottom. Honestly, I do not see how you can write a dissertation about the entrance into a destination that you say doesn't exist in the first place, but maybe I'm being too harsh. Obviously, I disagreed with the essay wholeheartedly, but then, that is his opinion, and I appreciate that. However, I did not appreciate the condescending tone toward those of us who do believe.

Not only do I believe I am going, but I also believe there will be loved ones, along with several dogs, waiting upon my glorious arrival.

Can I back my belief with absolute scientific fact? No, I can't. Does this make me somewhat intellectually inferior to him and others who do not share my thoughts? I would argue no. Again, I have no absolute facts on my side. But then, neither does he.

Simply put, we cannot use an earthly mind to comprehend a heavenly destination. To state facts about what awaits us based simply on your earthly knowledge is nothing more than speculation based upon speculation you've gleaned from other earthly minds.

I will say this, however, I have faith and the earthly mind of C.S. Lewis on my side ...I'll take that.

Tonight, we said good-bye to our sweet Lilly. She has gone on to a place where there are no thunderstorms, doggie biscuit trees line the streets, and a never-ending spring wind blows softly through her ears. She can just relax, lie there, and enjoy the wait.

Wait for me, Lillian, I'll see you again.

Yes, I most certainly will.

Epilogue

I finished this book two months ago; I promise I did.

I finished the project, a dream that I most assuredly did not possess as the year began. Some forty-six thousand words, and to be honest with you, I didn't know I could put that many down in some sort of coherent fashion, but a computer told me I did.

It was complete. All I had to do was simply hit one more key—tap a single key one final time—and send it to the editor. Just tap that key once, and those words, those words that so effortlessly at times slipped from me, those words would now be committed to the world wide inter-webs and land on another computer, in another city, for further review.

Hit that last key—blame it, that's the easy part. You would think.

I have been experiencing an inner battle for some reason. Some days I contemplated just tossing all these words and forgetting about it. I had simply wasted my time, and there was no use wasting any more. Who cares about that one great hot dog I had? Ducks, really? Oranges? Popcorn ceilings and wood-carving? My grandmother, my uncle, my father ...everyone has family. I had simply written stories that would serve as my own strange, self-written epitaph. Here's my life, yeah, I know, you had one too. No big deal.

I would put the book down and forget about it for days on end while I fought the battle. Truthfully, I have fought inner battles like this my whole life. The good thing about fighting those kinds of battles is you always win, but on the other hand, I guess you always lose as well.

I have been writing stories in some form or another for a good forty years. I would fill up composition books ...simply tossing them when there were no more clean sheets. I would stop for possibly years at a time. However, this jotting down of words accelerated back in the late nineties, when I was told by a very smart lady to write, just write ...and so I did once again.

There have been periods where the words would hurriedly escape from me onto defenseless paper. A torrent of feelings sprayed down like water on a bed of freshly planted flowers, or at times, acid onto those same works of His hand. These jottings, these transcriptions of my thoughts, had one thing in common ...they were always private. Words written seemingly just to myself. Some people talk to themselves; it seems I have preferred instead to write myself a note from time to time.

I began a couple of years ago tapping down these memories onto a keyboard and saving them. Dozens and dozens of stories from my life that I began earlier this year culling down to a somewhat manageable set, my hope being that maybe a book of my recollections and observations would find itself one day, at best, in a few bathrooms across the South. I most certainly do not possess delusions of grandeur, so, no coffee table resting spot ...the back of a few commodes would be sufficient for me.

I designed the front cover and back cover in less than an hour. I didn't go through several designs ...just one. It was easy—it was eerily simple.

Press the key, just press that key. I just couldn't do it, and now I know why.

The book was simply not complete.

My deepest thoughts, the most personal ones over the years, were most often reserved to talk about a lady. A lady who, to this day, the thought of her absence at times will conjure up that helpless, homesick feeling like a little kid at a never-ending summer camp. A kid who just wants to go home and see his mama.

Twenty years ago today, she passed away.

Mom was the sixth of seven children and the youngest of six daughters. A sometimes feisty woman, with Cherokee blood that flowed through every vein in her five-foot-and-a-few-inches body. She had skin that could tan at the simple mention of the sun and bare feet that could walk effortlessly across charred glass as though silk lined her path. She smoked Virginia Slims and drank Double Cola. She loved the telephone, flip-flops, and wouldn't even think about visiting the mailbox without her face fixed. She so loved her home but would find herself a self-induced prisoner in it for months on end and seemingly years at times. She would shake a lot during those periods. She never drank, and looking back, alcohol was never in the house. That house, her home …a home that had her mark on every square inch of livable space. She loved Elvis, my father, Conway Twitty, Burt Reynolds, dime stores, crafting, nighttime soaps, her poodle Bridget, Christmas, and me.

I should have included myself twice more on that list.

I feel like missing you today
Sometimes I just get this way
Seems like everything I see
Brings back another memory
I feel like missing you today

She left a month shy of her fifty-fourth year, and today, I am just a few months past that mark. Yes, it seems so much younger than it did twenty years ago. Now, each and every memory that I have of her, I must realize she was in fact younger than I am at this very moment.

It takes a bit of getting used to.

Truthfully, I realize that I am much older than my mind has been telling me all this time. It's kinda funny—all these years I've felt much younger than the school buddies I would see out from time to time. This is yet another reason that I have always felt that mirrors are liars. Let's face it—a reflection is simply an opposite representation.

I guess catching up with a parent on a timeline has that effect on a person.

I often laugh when I hear the phrase *mama's boy*. I have always felt that descriptive was most obviously coined back in the late sixties to describe that boy over there on Lewis Street's undying devotion. Up until then, boys loved their mothers, I'm most assured they did ...but seemingly, my devotion reached biblical levels. A term had to be developed, and so it was. That's right. I was the very first one ...the Neil Armstrong, if you will, of boys who still desperately cling to a seemingly invisible umbilical cord.

She loved me, her only child, so intensely that to this day I can almost wrap myself up in it like a thick quilt and find comfort on a chilly winter night.

I believe I received the ability to write from my dad, but the desire came from my mom.

She didn't deserve those last few years. She didn't deserve to hear the word *cancer*. She didn't deserve the fear it brings, all the pain and all that sickness. She didn't deserve to simply evaporate in front of our eyes.

Angels don't deserve hell.

You're never too far from my mind
I feel like crying sometimes
It's always been so hard to do
Especially when it comes to you
You're never too far from my mind

I am fully aware that "His ways are not ours" and that "He works in mysterious ways." I do not and will not question Him. But, just because I do not question does not mean I understand and that I accept it. It means I am simply going on and looking toward that day when I don't have to hurt on Mother's Day anymore.

I know someday I'll see your smiling face again
I don't know when, but I know it's true
One other thing I know
No matter where we go
You love me, and I love you

"Missing You" by Todd Snider

Love you Mama.

• • •

I think it's time to hit that key.

About the Author

Dale Forrester grew up in Rossville, Georgia. He began his advertising career shortly after graduating from the University of Tennessee at Chattanooga with a B.S. in Marketing.

Over the years, he has garnered numerous industry awards for graphic design, copywriting, audio and video production and photography on the local level, as well as both regionally and nationally.

Today, he lives in Chickamauga, Georgia, with his wife Laura and two children, Corey and Kirby nearby.

For more information, please visit his website at www. LivingMyDays.com.

About the Type

This book was set in Goudy Old Style, a typeface developed by the legendary Frederic Goudy. Goudy Old Style was released in 1915 and became an instant classic. It remains to this day his most memorable typeface design.

Mr. Goudy began his career in 1903 in Park Ridge, Illinois in partnership with Will Ransom. Their company, Village Press, later moved to Boston and finally New York. He created his first significant typeface, often referred to as Goudy Light, in 1908 for the Lanston Monotype Machine Company. It was later that same year that a fire totally consumed Village Press destroying all of the equipment and all of his designs. Mr. Goudy's career was seemingly over.

An article written by Andrew R. Boone for Popular Science in their April, 1942 issue, contains this passage:

"At 40, this short, plump, pinkish, and puckish gentleman kept books for a Chicago realtor and considered himself a failure.

During the next 36 years, starting almost from scratch at an age when most men are permanently set in their chosen vocations, he cut 113 fonts of type, thereby creating more usable faces than did the seven greatest inventors of type and books, from Gutenberg to Garamond."

Yes, Mr. Goudy could have simply gone on with his life and not pursued his passion any longer, but he somehow found the will to get back at it again. I look at him as not only an artist, but also a source of inspiration. I'm proud to showcase some of his work in this book.